1001

FUNNIEST

THINGS
EVER SAID

1001
FUNNIEST
THINGS
EVER SAID

Edited by
Steven D. Price

THE LYONS PRESS
Guilford, Connecticut
An imprint of The Globe Pequot Press

Copyright © 2006 by Steven D. Price

ALL RIGHTS RESERVED. No part of this book may be reproduced or transmitted in any form by any means, electronic or mechanical, including photocopying and recording, or by any information storage and retrieval system, except as may be expressly permitted in writing from the publisher. Requests for permission should be addressed to The Lyons Press, Attn: Rights and Permissions Department, P.O. Box 480, Guilford, CT 06437.

The Lyons Press is an imprint of The Globe Pequot Press.

10 9 8 7 6 5 4 3 2 1

Printed in the United States of America

Designed by Carol Sawyer/Rose Design

ISBN 13: 978-1-59228-443-6

ISBN 10: 1-59228-443-4

Library of Congress Cataloging-in-Publication Data is available on file.

CONTENTS

A smile is an inexpensive way to improve your looks.

—*Charles Gordy*

INTRODUCTION

Cee

What is "funny?" Literary critics, philosophers, psychologists, and social commentators have struggled for a definition since the ancients tackled the question. Although there have been as many theories as people who advanced them, several of them provide a useful overview:

The first variety of humor that we encounter in life is referred to as the humor of the forbidden, an elegant way of saying "potty jokes." Kids are taught that jokes about bodily functions are "no-no's" in polite society (whatever "polite society" now means), as is sex when they learn the facts of life. To assert their independence as well as to get a sure-fire laugh from playmates, children joke about things that they've been told not to talk about. This preoccupation with "naughty" themes continues throughout life, which accounts for adult humor's popularity and enduring appeal.

Although we feel a kind of personal empowerment when we violate such social codes, that's not what's meant by "humor of superiority." That phrase refers to the joke-teller, and by implication the audience, feeling intellectually or morally better than the joke's subject, whether the butt of the joke is a nationality or ethnic group, a certain class or group (e.g., dumb blondes), or a figment of the imagination ("Yo' Mama"). You and I would never be so stupid as the person in the joke, and that's largely why we find it so funny.

Superiority humor raises the issue of taste and/or decency, which we might as well address right now. Putting someone down only on the strength of race, religion, or national origin is in several senses a cheap shot. However, such jokes and comments are widespread, and truth be told, they can also be very funny. Since the purpose of this book is to enshrine—if that's the right word—funny things that people have said, we made a decision not to exclude those kinds of jokes. However, you'll find nothing patently offensive.

One person's sense of superiority is another's effort at survival, and many ethnic groups view put-downs or at least self-deprecating jokes as a way to keep some semblance of balance in a brutally unfunny world. Many jokes are intended for only the group in question and include the use of words that would be termed offensive epithets if used by an outsider. Others poke fun somewhat more gently at oppressors, such as the Native American jibe that "When Columbus landed, one Native American turned to another and said, 'Well, there goes the neighborhood.'"

Okay, that's when and how we laugh, but *why* do we laugh? What makes something funny? The wit of verbal gymnastics make us laugh in appreciation, a sort of vocal applause. When asked to distinguish between a misfortune and a calamity, British Prime Minister Benjamin Disraeli's reply that "If Mr. Gladstone fell into the Thames, that would be a misfortune; if someone pulled him out, that would be a calamity" is witty, and we respond to the verbal gymnastic with a chuckle (knowing about the fierce rivalry between Disraeli and Gladstone adds to our appreciation).

We also laugh at the unexpected, such as Woody Allen's observation that "Not only is there no God, but try getting a plumber on weekends." And at the absurd: Steven Wright's remark that "I knew these Siamese twins. They moved to England, so the other one could drive."

Whatever, however, why ever . . . we love to laugh, and for good reason. Humor is both emotionally and physically beneficial; *Reader's Digest* has a feature called "Laughter Is the Best Medicine," and doctors agree that it is. The ancients believed that our bodies were composed of four humors, or fluids, that had to be kept in balance to maintain health. One of the humors was sanguine, coming from the word for "blood" and now meaning cheerfully optimistic, a concept that's very close to being amused. Today's physicians understand that laughter lowers blood pressure, reduces stress, elevates mood, boosts the immune system, establishes social connections with others, and— best of all—makes us feel good.

Two parting pieces of advice: first, don't try to convince someone that a humorous item is indeed funny if the person doesn't find it so. It just won't work, for as Shakespeare put it, "a jest's prosperity lies in the ear of him that hears it, never in the tongue of him that makes it." Then too, never tell someone that he or she has no sense of humor. We can tolerate almost every kind of criticism or slur, but to be told we have no sense of humor is fighting words.

But not you—you have a terrific sense of humor. So read on, and laugh at these goodies. You'll love them. You can trust me. . . . I mean, have I ever lied to you before?

To all the people who suggested entries for this collection, I tip my fool's cap. Ditto to all the authors and entertainers who have made me laugh over the years. And to all the others, beginning with my father Martin Price and including but not limited to Dr. Jeff Buckner, Rick Berman, Melanie Garnett, Judy Goldman, Rich Goldman, William Gordon, Joan Hansen, Steve Khinoy, Richard Liebmann-Smith, Gil Musinger, Jan Petersen, Cynthia Peraner, Gail Weinberg, Norton Wolf, and Dave Wright.

Finally, as ever, special thanks to my editor, colleague, and friend Holly Rubino.

STEVEN D. PRICE
NEW YORK, NEW YORK
JULY 2006

THE FUNNY MEN
MEN
AND
WOMEN

"Take My Wife . . . . Please!"

BOB HOPE

Bob Hope was the reigning stand-up comedian for much of the twentieth century, whether in movies, on radio and TV or entertaining the troops during wartime. His fixation with golf was an integral part of his life . . . and art.

Players occasionally have to contend with these gusty desert winds. I hit a ball into the wind one day . . . but I shouldn't have watched it with my mouth open. I'm the only guy around here with an Adam's Apple marked Spalding Kro-Flite.
>   *—on an incident that occurred to him one year at La Quinta and left him speechless—if you can believe it*

Incidentally, the toughest parts of the course for me nowadays are the sand traps. It's not hard to get the ball out . . . the problem is to get me out, at my age.

I set out to play golf with the intention of shooting my age, but I shot my weight instead.

I asked my good friend, Arnold Palmer, how I could improve my game, he advised me to cheat.

I've played some strange rounds of golf in my travels. One course in Alaska was hacked out of the wilderness. My caddy was a moose. Every time I reached for a club he thought I was trying to steal his antlers.

The Scottish caddies are great. One old fellow at St. Andrews told me, "I had a golfer who was so lousy he threw his clubs into the water. Then he dived in himself. I thought he was going to drown, but I remembered he couldn't keep his head down long enough."

Jimmy Stewart could have been a good golfer, but he speaks so slowly that by the time he yells "Fore!" the guy he's hit is already in an ambulance on the way to the hospital.

HOPE

Oscar night at my house is called Passover.
> —*joking about the fact that he has never won an Oscar for his acting abilities*

You should have seen the Christmas cards I got this year. I got one card from Marilyn Monroe with a picture of her in a bathing suit. What a picture. You know how George Washington looks straight ahead on a two-cent stamp. Well, on this envelope, he kept peeking over his shoulder.

I wouldn't exactly say that Hollywood Boulevard is crowded with Christmas shoppers . . . but when I was driving, I put my arm out to make a turn . . . and when I took it back in, it was gift-wrapped.

But the crowds were very friendly . . . honestly . . . it was the pleasantest mob I ever lost a tooth in.

It's so crowded in Los Angeles these days . . . if you get a sunburn you have to go to Glendale to peel.

My brother was a musician. His favorite was small combinations. He used to hum while he broke them open.

A James Cagney love scene is one where he lets the other guy live.

W. C. Fields

The legendary film, vaudeville, and radio curmudgeon and tippler with the bulbous nose and rotund body who said that "anyone who hates children and animals can't be all bad."

W. C. Fields appeared on the program with ventriloquist Edgar Bergen with whose dummy, Charlie McCarthy, Fields had a running feud. Fields smuggled a saw on stage and, as a stunned Bergen looked on, finally cut his adversary down to size. "I'll always have a warm place for you, Charlie," Fields said.

"Where?" Charlie asked. "In your heart?"

"No, in my fireplace."

I was married once—in San Francisco. I haven't seen her for many years. The great earthquake and fire in 1906 destroyed the marriage certificate. There's no legal proof. Which proves that earthquakes aren't all bad.

I have been asked if I ever get the DTs; I don't know; it's hard to tell where Hollywood ends and the DTs begin.

If at first you don't succeed, try, try, and try again. Then give up. There's no use being a damned fool about it.

Madam, there's no such thing as a tough child—if you parboil them first for seven hours, they always come out tender.

A woman drove me to drink—and I hadn't even the courtesy to thank her.

GEORGE BURNS

With his wife Gracie Allen and his ever-present cigar, Burns was a popular figure on radio and TV, living to age 100 and working almost until his death.

First you forget names, then you forget faces. Next you forget to pull your zipper up and finally, you forget to pull it down.

A good sermon should have a good beginning and a good ending, and they should be as close together as possible.

Happiness? A good cigar, a good meal, a good cigar and a good woman—or a bad woman; it depends on how much happiness you can handle.

Jack [Benny] was tremendously talented, and I can honestly say I've never heard anyone play the violin the way he did. And I'll always be grateful for that, too.

I was married by a judge. I should have asked for a jury.

Actually, it only takes one drink to get me loaded. Trouble is, I can't remember if it's the thirteenth or fourteenth.

B

U

R

N

S

JACK BENNY

A star of radio and TV, Benny was well known for his supposed stinginess and less-than-virtuoso violin playing.

Jack Benny is walking down the street, when a stick-up man pulls out a gun and says, "Your money or your life!" An extremely long silence follows. "Your money or your life!" the thug repeats.

Finally Benny says, "I'm thinking!"

I don't want to tell you how much insurance I carry with the Prudential, but all I can say is: when I go, they go too.

Give me golf clubs, fresh air and a beautiful partner, and you can keep the clubs and the fresh air.

Any man who would walk five miles through the snow, barefoot, just to return a library book so he could save three cents—that's my kind of guy.

—*about Abraham Lincoln*

It's a real Strad, you know. If it isn't I'm out one hundred and ten dollars. The reason I got it so cheap is that it's one of the few Strads made in Japan.

—*about his fiddle*

I don't deserve this award, but I have arthritis and I don't deserve that either.

The last time I got a standing ovation was in England when I played with the London Philharmonic. I played the Wieniawski Concerto, and when I finished, the whole audience stood up and walked out!

B
E
N
N
Y

Henny Youngman

The king of the one-liners, Youngman is best known for his "Take my wife . . . please!" signature joke.

The patient says, "Doctor, it hurts when I do this."

The doctor replies, "Then don't do that!"

The doctor says to the patient, "Take your clothes off and stick your tongue out the window."

"What will that do?" asks the patient.

The doctor says, "I'm mad at my neighbor!"

Getting on a plane, I told the ticket lady, "Send one of my bags to New York, send one to Los Angeles, and send one to Miami."

She said, "We can't do that!"

I told her, "You did it last week!"

A father is explaining ethics to his son, who is about to go into business: "Suppose a woman comes in and orders a hundred dollars' worth of material. You wrap it up, and you give it to her. She pays you with a $100 bill. But as she goes out the door you realize she's given you two $100 bills. Now, here's where the ethics come in: Should you or should you not tell your partner?"

Someone stole all my credit cards, but I won't be reporting it. The thief spends less than my wife did.

I take my wife everywhere, but she keeps finding her way back.

I asked my wife, "Where do you want to go for our anniversary?"

She said, "Somewhere I have never been!"

I told her, "How about the kitchen?"

YOUNGMAN

I played a lot of tough clubs in my time. Once a guy in one of those clubs wanted to bet me $10 that I was dead. I was afraid to bet.

A woman in a bar says to a man, "I haven't seen you around here."

The man replies, "Yes, I just got out of jail for killing my wife."

The woman says, "Oh, so you're single. . . ."

Rodney Dangerfield

Dangerfield's night club routine was based on his "I don't get no respect" inferiority complex.

I went to the psychiatrist, and he says, "You're crazy."

I tell him I want a second opinion.

He says, "Okay, you're ugly too!"

I told my psychiatrist that everyone hates me. He said I was being ridiculous—everyone hasn't met me yet.

With my wife I don't get no respect. I made a toast on her birthday to "the best woman a man ever had." The waiter joined me.

D
A
N
G
E
R
F
I
E
L
D

I'm not a sexy guy. I went to a hooker. I dropped my pants. She dropped her price.

What a childhood I had. Why, when I took my first step, my old man tripped me!

Last week I told my psychiatrist, "I keep thinking about suicide." He told me from now on I have to pay in advance.

I tell ya when I was a kid, all I knew was rejection. My yo-yo, it never came back!

I tell you, with my doctor, I don't get no respect. I told him, "I've swallowed a bottle of sleeping pills." He told me to have a few drinks and get some rest.

With my dog I don't get no respect. He keeps barking at the front door. He don't want to go out. He wants me to leave.

What a dog I got. His favorite bone is in my arm!

Last week I saw my psychiatrist. I told him, "Doc, I keep thinking I'm a dog." He told me to get off his couch.

I worked in a pet store and people kept asking how big I'd get.

D
A
N
G
E
R
F
I
E
L
D

Joan Rivers

A popular TV and night club personality, Joan Rivers is known for her unsparingly acid tongue.

Boy George is all England needs—another queen who can't dress.

I hate housework. You make the beds, you wash the dishes and six months later you have to start all over again.

I knew I was an unwanted baby when I saw that my bath toys were a toaster and a radio.

I told my mother-in-law that my house was her house, and she said, "Get the hell off my property."

If God wanted us to bend over he'd put diamonds on the floor.

Is Elizabeth Taylor fat? Her favorite food is seconds.

My mother could make anybody feel guilty—she used to get letters
of apology from people she didn't even know.

R
I
V
E
R
S

DICK GREGORY

One of the first African-American stand-up comedians to speak out on race and civil rights issues.

Good evening, ladies and gentlemen. I understand there are a good many Southerners in the room tonight. I know the South very well. I spent twenty years there one night.

Last time I was down South I walked into this restaurant and this white waitress came up to me and said, "We don't serve colored people here."

I said, "That's all right. I don't eat colored people. Bring me a whole fried chicken."

Then these three white boys came up to me and said, "Boy, we're givin' you fair warnin'. Anything you do to that chicken, we're gonna do to you."

So I put down my knife and fork, I picked up that chicken and I kissed it. Then I said, "Line up, boys!"

Baseball is very big with my people. It figures. It's the only way we can get to shake a bat at a white man without starting a riot.

I never believed in Santa Claus because I knew no white dude would come into my neighborhood after dark.

~

STEVEN WRIGHT

The absolute master of absurdities and far-out concepts.

I went for a walk last night and my girlfriend asked me how long I was going to be gone. I said, "The whole time."

I used to work in a fire hydrant factory. You couldn't park anywhere near the place.

I replaced the headlights on my car with strobe lights. Now it looks like I'm the only one moving.

I knew these Siamese twins. They moved to England, so the other one could drive.

I went to a restaurant with a sign that said they served breakfast at any time. So I ordered French toast during the Renaissance.

W
R
I
G
H
T

WOODY ALLEN

Allen's intellectual loser persona made the transition from stand-up comedy to successful films.

My love life is terrible. The last time I was inside a woman was when I visited the Statue of Liberty.

Not only is there no God, but try getting a plumber on weekends.

It's not that I'm afraid to die. I just don't want to be there when it happens.

I am at two with nature.

Some guy hit my fender, and I told him, "Be fruitful, and multiply."
But not in those words.

I don't want to achieve immortality through my work. . . . I want to
achieve it through not dying.

I took a speed reading course and read *War and Peace* in twenty
minutes. It's about Russia.

A
L
L
E
N

ROBIN WILLIAMS

Manic and wildly inventive, Williams may well possess the world's quickest wit.

God gave men both a penis and a brain, but unfortunately not enough blood supply to run both at the same time.

We had gay burglars the other night. They broke in and rearranged the furniture.

If it's the Psychic Network why do they need a phone number?

PAUL LYNDE

Lynde made his mark as the slyly fey "center square" on the TV quiz show Hollywood Squares.

Peter Marshall [host]: If the right part comes along, will George C. Scott do a nude scene?

Paul Lynde: You mean he doesn't have the right part?

Peter Marshall: In *Alice in Wonderland*, who kept crying, "I'm late, I'm late?"

Paul Lynde: Alice, and her mother is sick about it.

Peter Marshall: Paul, why do Hell's Angels wear leather?

Paul Lynde: Because chiffon wrinkles too easily.

Peter Marshall: True or false . . . research indicates that Columbus liked to wear bloomers and long stockings.

Paul Lynde: It's not easy to sign a crew up for six months. . . .

Peter Marshall: It is considered in bad taste to discuss two subjects at nudist camps. One is politics. What is the other?

Paul Lynde: Tape measures.

Peter Marshall: When you pat a dog on its head he will usually wag his tail. What will a goose do?

Paul Lynde: Make him bark.

Peter Marshall: Billy Graham recently called it "our great hope in a confusing and ever-changing world." What is it?

Paul Lynde: Pampers.

Peter Marshall: Is it normal for Norwegians to talk to trees?

Paul Lynde: As long as that's as far as it goes.

Peter Marshall: If you were pregnant for two years, what would you give birth to?

Paul Lynde: Whatever it is, it would never be afraid of the dark.

Peter Marshall: What should you do if you're going 55 miles per hour and your tires suddenly blow out?

Paul Lynde: Honk if you believe in Jesus.

Groucho Marx

The raffish roué and verbal gymnast Groucho went from Marx Brothers films to the hit TV show, You Bet Your Life.

From the moment I picked your book up until I laid it down, I was convulsed with laughter. Someday I intend reading it.

I didn't like the play, but then I saw it under adverse conditions—the curtain was up.

I never forget a face, but in your case I'll be glad to make an exception.

I refuse to join any club that would have me as a member.

Outside of a dog, a book is a man's best friend. Inside of a dog it's too dark to read.

Room service? Send up a larger room.

She got her looks from her father. He's a plastic surgeon.

Why, a four-year-old child could understand this report. Run out and find me a four-year-old child. I can't make head nor tail out of it.

Why should I care about posterity? What's posterity ever done for me?

MARX

M
A
R
X

Why, I'd horse-whip you if I had a horse.

My daughter is half-Jewish, can she wade in up to her knees?
—when told that a swimming pool
was off-limits to Jews

DOROTHY PARKER

One of the Algonquin Hotel "Round Table" wits, Parker wrote short stories and screenplays.

Money cannot buy health, but I'd settle for a diamond-studded wheelchair.

The two most beautiful words in the English language are "cheque enclosed."

If you want to know what God thinks of money, just look at the people he gave it to.

P

A

R

K

E

R

P

A

R   That woman speaks eighteen languages, and can't say no in any
of them.

K

E   You can lead a horticulture, but you can't make her think.

R

This is not a novel to be tossed aside lightly. It should be thrown
with great force.

If all the young ladies who attended the Yale prom were laid end to
end, no one would be the least surprised.

When someone said, "I really can't come to your party Mrs. Parker.
I can't bear fools."

Parker replied, "That's strange; your mother could."

GEORGE CARLIN

An iconoclast, Carlin is known for verbal gymnastics and testing the limits of tolerated language.

Have you ever noticed? Anybody going slower than you is an idiot, and anyone going faster than you is a maniac.

We ought to have a diet salad dressing called "500 Islands."

When a ghostwriter dies, how many people come back?

I recently bought a book of free verse. For twelve dollars.

Why do they bother saying "raw sewage"? Do some people actually cook that stuff?

EMO PHILIPS

Philips is known for his eccentric appearance, falsetto voice, and outlandish humor.

A computer once beat me at chess, but it was no match for me at kick boxing.

When I was a kid I used to pray every night for a new bicycle. Then I realized that the Lord doesn't work that way so I stole one and asked Him to forgive me.

You know what I hate? Indian givers . . . no, I take that back.

I was walking down Fifth Avenue today and I found a wallet, and I was gonna keep it, rather than return it, but I thought: well, if I lost a hundred and fifty dollars, how would I feel? And I realized I would want to be taught a lesson.

How many people here have telekenetic powers? Raise my hand.

I got in a fight one time with a really big guy, and he said, "I'm going to mop the floor with your face."

I said, "You'll be sorry."

He said, "Oh, yeah? Why?"

I said, "Well, you won't be able to get into the corners very well."

SPIKE MILLIGAN

A member of Britain's Goon Show *troupe, Milligan was voted in a BBC poll "the funniest person of the last 1,000 years."*

How long was I in the army? Five foot eleven.

I speak Esparanto like a native.

A sure cure for seasickness is to sit under a tree.

I thought I'd begin by reading a poem by Shakespeare, but then I thought, why should I? He never reads any of mine.

ERMA BOMBECK

A newspaper and magazine columnist, Bombeck is adept at finding the humor in everyday life.

Do you know what you call those who use towels and never wash them, eat meals and never do the dishes, sit in rooms they never clean, and are entertained till they drop? If you have just answered, "A houseguest," you're wrong because I have just described my kids.

Getting out of the hospital is a lot like resigning from a book club. You're not out of it until the computer says you're out of it.

God created man, but I could do better.

Have you any idea how many kids it takes to turn off one light in the kitchen? Three. It takes one to say, "What light?" and two more to say, "I didn't turn it on."

B
O
M
B
E
C
K

B

O

M

B

E

C

K

It goes without saying that you should never have more children than you have car windows.

Making coffee has become the great compromise of the decade. It's the only thing "real" men do that doesn't seem to threaten their masculinity. To women, it's on the same domestic entry level as putting the spring back into the toilet-tissue holder or taking a chicken out of the freezer to thaw.

My kids always perceived the bathroom as a place where you wait it out until all the groceries are unloaded from the car.

FRED ALLEN

A literate and absurdist radio comedian, Allen hosted a long-running radio show. His comic feud with Jack Benny was one hallmark of his humor.

I always have trouble remembering three things: faces, names, and—I can't remember what the third thing is.

I can't understand why a person will take a year to write a novel when he can easily buy one for a few dollars.

I like long walks, especially when they are taken by people who annoy me.

I'd rather have a full bottle in front of me than a full frontal lobotomy.

I'm a little hoarse tonight. I've been living in Chicago for the past two months, and you know how it is, yelling for help on the way home every night. Things are so tough in Chicago that at Easter time, for bunnies the little kids use porcupines.

Life, in my estimation, is a biological misadventure that we terminate on the shoulders of six strange men whose only objective is to make a hole in one with you.

Television is a medium because anything well done is rare.

The first thing that strikes a visitor to Paris is a taxi.

The last time I saw him he was walking down lover's lane holding his own hand.

You can take all the sincerity in Hollywood, place it in the navel of a fruit fly and still have room enough for three caraway seeds and a producer's heart.

My mom said she learned how to swim. Someone took her out in the lake and threw her off the boat. That's how she learned how to swim.

I said, "Mom, they weren't trying to teach you how to swim."
—*Paula Poundstone*

Ever wonder if illiterate people get the full effect of alphabet soup?
—*John Mendoza*

Relationships are hard. It's like a full-time job, and we should treat it like one. If your boyfriend or girlfriend wants to leave you, they should give you two weeks' notice. There should be severance pay, and before they leave you, they should have to find you a temp.
—*Bob Ettinger*

A study in the *Washington Post* says that women have better verbal skills than men. I just want to say to the authors of that study: Duh.

—*Conan O'Brien*

Who picks your clothes—Stevie Wonder?

—*Don Rickles to David Letterman*

My grandfather's a little forgetful, but he likes to give me advice. One day, he took me aside and left me there.

—*Ron Richards*

I was a vegetarian until I started leaning towards sunlight.

—*Rita Rudner*

The Swiss have an interesting army. Five hundred years without a war. Pretty impressive. Also pretty lucky for them. Ever see that little Swiss Army knife they have to fight with? Not much of a weapon there. Corkscrews. Bottle openers. "Come on, buddy, let's go. You get past me, the guy in back of me, he's got a spoon. Back off. I've got the toe clippers right here."

—*Jerry Seinfeld*

The president boasted at the top of his press conference that we have the support now of Britain and Spain for our attack on Iraq. You know, when you want to make it perfectly clear to the world that you're not an imperialist, the people you want in your corner are Britain and Spain.

—*Bill Maher*

I don't kill flies but I like to mess with their minds. I hold them above globes. They freak out and yell, "Whoa, I'm way too high!"

—*Bruce Baum*

Why does Sea World have a seafood restaurant? I'm halfway through my fishburger and I realize, Oh my God. . . . I could be eating a slow learner.

—*Lynda Montgomery*

I won't say ours was a tough school, but we had our own coroner. We used to write essays like: What I'm going to be if I grow up.

—*Lenny Bruce*

I don't like country music, but I don't mean to denigrate those who do. And for the people who like country music, denigrate means "put down."

—*Bob Newhart*

While visiting Venice for the first time, Robert Benchley sent a telegram to Harold Ross, his editor at *The New Yorker*. "Streets full of water," the cable read. "Please advise."

Leaving the Algonquin Hotel one evening, a well-lubricated Robert Benchley found himself face to face with a uniformed man whom he took to be the doorman. "Would you get me a taxi, my good man?" Benchley requested.

"Now see here," the man proudly replied, "I happen to be a rear admiral in the United States navy."

"Perfectly all right," Benchley nonchalantly replied. "Just get me a battleship then."

I'm always amazed to hear of air crash victims so badly mutilated that they have to be identified by their dental records. What I can't understand is, if they don't know who you are, how do they know who your dentist is?

—*Paul Merton*

There is one thing I would break up over and that is if she caught me
with another woman. I wouldn't stand for that.

—*Steve Martin*

I'm desperately trying to figure out why kamikaze pilots
wore helmets.

—*Dave Edison*

Now they show you how detergents take out bloodstains, a pretty
violent image there. I think if you've got a T-shirt with a bloodstain
all over it, maybe laundry isn't your biggest problem. Maybe you
should get rid of the body before you do the wash.

—*Jerry Seinfeld*

Oh my God, look at you. Anyone else hurt in the accident?

—*Don Rickles to Ernest Borgnine*

Tragedy is when I cut my finger. Comedy is when you fall into an open sewer and die.

—*Mel Brooks*

My grandfather always said, "Don't watch your money; watch your health." So one day while I was watching my health, someone stole my money. It was my grandfather.

—*Jackie Mason*

A Jewish grandmother is watching her grandchild playing on the beach when a huge wave comes and takes him out to sea. She pleads, "Please God, save my only grandson. I beg of you, bring him back." And a big wave comes and washes the boy back onto the beach, good as new. She looks up to heaven and says, "He had a hat!"

—*Myron Cohen*

I celebrated Thanksgiving in an old-fashioned way. I invited everyone in my neighborhood to my house, we had an enormous feast, and then I killed them and took their land.

—*Jon Stewart*

The guy who shot Robert Kennedy, Sirhan Sirhan, goes up for parole every year. Once he even told the parole board that if Kennedy was alive today, he would speak in his favor and say let him go. What a tough break, you know? The one guy who would have supported Sirhan, and he shot him.

—*Paula Poundstone*

The Dalai Lama visited the White House and told the president that he could teach him to find a higher state of consciousness. Then after talking to Bush for a few minutes, he said, "You know what? Let's just grab lunch."

—*Bill Maher*

The trouble with unemployment is that the minute you wake up in the morning you're on the job.

Slappy White

One of my uncles who watches a boxing match with me always says, "Sure. Ten million dollars. You know, for that kind of money, I'd fight him." As if someone is going to pay $200 a ticket to see a 57-year-old carpet salesman get hit in the face once and cry.

—*Larry Miller*

If variety is the spice of life, marriage is the big can of leftover Spam.

—*Johnny Carson*

I think men who have a pierced ear are better prepared for marriage.
They've experienced pain and bought jewelry.

—*Rita Rudner*

Any time a person goes into a delicatessen and orders a pastrami on
white bread, somewhere a Jew dies.

—*Milton Berle*

When Mel [Brooks] told his Jewish mother he was marrying an
Italian girl, she said, "Bring her over. I'll be in the kitchen—with
my head in the oven."

—*Anne Bancroft*

She's a lovely person. She deserves a good husband. Marry her before she finds one.
            —*Oscar Levant to Harpo Marx upon meeting Harpo's fiancée*

My husband was so ugly, he used to stand outside the doctor's office and make people sick.

                              —*Jackie "Moms" Mabley*

Always be nice to your children because they are the ones who will choose your rest home.

                              —*Phyllis Diller*

Experts say you should never hit your children in anger. When is a good time? When you're feeling festive?

—*Roseanne Barr*

Then there was the idiot accountant who became an embezzler. He ran away with the accounts payable.

—*Jackie Mason*

Health nuts are going to feel stupid someday, lying in hospitals dying of nothin'.

—*Redd Foxx*

My doctor is wonderful. Once when I couldn't afford an operation, he touched up the X-rays.

—*Joey Bishop*

The problem with the designated driver program, it's not a desirable job. But if you ever get sucked into doing it, have fun with it. At the end of the night, drop them off at the wrong house.

—*Jeff Foxworthy*

Most turkeys taste better the day after; my mother's tasted better the day before.

—*Rita Rudner*

My doctor told me that jogging could add years to my life. He was right. I feel ten years older already.

—*Milton Berle*

Don't let a man put anything over on you except an umbrella.

—*Mae West*

We have women in the military, but they don't put us in the front lines. They don't know if we can fight, if we can kill. I think we can. All the general has to do is walk over to the women and say, "You see the enemy over there? They say you look fat in those uniforms."

—*Elayne Boosler*

We were so poor my daddy unplugged the clocks when we went
to bed.

—*Chris Rock*

Advice to children crossing the street: Damn the lights. Watch the
cars. The lights ain't never killed nobody.

—*Jackie "Moms" Mabley*

A wedding is a funeral where you smell your own flowers.

—*Eddie Cantor*

II

SPORTS CAPERS

Casey Stengel Would Be Spinning in His Grave

YOGI BERRA

An all-star catcher with the New York Yankees and then manager of both the Yankees and the New York Mets, Berra is well known for his wonderful and deceptively simple use of the English language.

This is like déjà vu all over again.

I don't know if it's good for baseball, but it sure beats the hell out of rooming with Phil Rizzuto.

> *—on being told that Joe DiMaggio*
> *was to marry Marilyn Monroe*

You better cut the pizza in four pieces because I'm not hungry enough to eat six.

Thanks, you don't look so hot yourself.

> *—after being told he looked cool*

B
E
R
R
A

Yeah, but we're making great time!
                    —in response to "Hey Yogi, I think we're lost"

Nobody goes there anymore; it's too crowded.

It gets late early out there.
                    —referring to the bad sun conditions
                    in left field at the stadium

If the fans don't come out to the ball park, you can't stop them.

Why buy good luggage? You only use it when you travel.

How long have you known me, Jack? And you still don't know how
to spell my name.
                    —when he received a check made out to "bearer"

B
E
R
R
A

B

E

R

R

A

I never blame myself when I'm not hitting. I just blame the bat, and if it keeps up, I change bats. After all, if I know it isn't my fault that I'm not hitting, how can I get mad at myself?

You should always go to other people's funerals; otherwise, they won't come to yours.

I didn't really say everything I said.

CASEY STENGEL

Manager of the New York Yankees and New York Mets, Stengel's "amazin'"
convoluted utterances made him one of baseball's most colorful figures.

All right, everybody line up alphabetically according to your height.

I couldn't have done it without my players.
                              —on winning the 1958 World Series

The team has come along slow but fast.

Good pitching will always stop good hitting and vice-versa.

You have to have a catcher because if you don't you're likely to have
a lot of passed balls.

S
T
E
N
G
E
L

I was such a dangerous hitter I even got intentional walks in batting practice.

Left-handers have more enthusiasm for life. They sleep on the wrong side of the bed and their head gets more stagnant on that side.

It's wonderful to meet so many friends that I didn't used to like.

There comes a time in every man's life and I've had plenty of them.

Ralph Kiner

Former Pittsburgh Pirates outfielder Kiner went on to a career in radio and television broadcasting.

Hello, everybody. Welcome to Kiner's Corner. This is . . . uh. I'm . . . uh . . .

All of his saves have come in relief appearances.

All of the Mets' road wins against the Dodgers this year occurred at Dodger Stadium.

If Casey Stengel were alive today, he'd be spinning in his grave.

Kevin McReynolds stops at third—and he scores!

On Father's Day, we again wish you all happy birthday.

Solo homers usually come with no one on base.

The Hall of Fame ceremonies are on the thirty-first and thirty-second of July.

The Mets have gotten their leadoff batter on only once this inning.

There's a lot of heredity in that family.

Tony Gwynn was named player of the year for April.

RON FAIRLY

A first baseman and outfielder for several teams, Fairly is now a sportscaster on the West Coast.

Bruce Sutter has been around for a while and he's pretty old. He's thirty-five years old. That will give you some idea of how old he is.

He fakes a bluff.

I hit one that far (said after seeing a Mike Schmidt home run) once and I still bogeyed the hole.

Last night I neglected to mention something that bears repeating.

The wind at Candlestick tonight is blowing with great propensity.

JERRY COLEMAN

After playing second base for the New York Yankees, Coleman went on to broadcast games for the San Diego Padres.

He (Graig Nettles) leaped up to make one of those diving stops only he can make.

He slides into second with a stand-up double.

Larry Lintz steals second standing up—he slid, but he didn't have to.

(Willie) McCovey swings and misses, and it's fouled back.

Rich Folkers is throwing up in the bullpen.

There's someone warming up in the bullpen, but he's obscured by his number.

They throw (Dave) Winfield out at second—and he's safe.

Trailing 5–1, the Padres added an insurance run in the eighth inning.

That home run ties it up, 1–0.

When you lose your hands, you can't play baseball.

That big guy, Winfield, at 6'6", can do things only a small man can do.

C
O
L
E
M
A
N

Ozzie Smith just made another play that I've never seen anyone else make before, and I've seen him make it more often than anyone else ever has.

Sunday is Senior Citizens' Day. And if you want to become a senior citizen, just call the Padre ticket office.

I've never seen a game like this. Every game this year has been like this.

(Dave) Winfield goes back to the wall, he hits his head on the wall and it rolls off! It's rolling all the way back to second base. This is a terrible thing for the Padres.

DIZZY DEAN

An American League pitcher who became the prototype of English-mangling broadcasters during the 1940s and '50s.

He (Branch Rickey) must think I went to the Massachusetts Constitution of Technology.

The doctors x-rayed my head and found nothing.

Well what's wrong with "ain't"? And as for saying (Phil) Rizzuto slud into second, it just ain't natural. Sounds silly to me. Slud is something more than slid. It means sliding with great effort.

A lot of folks who ain't sayin' "ain't," ain't eatin'. So, Teach, you learn 'em English, and I'll learn 'em baseball.
> —*reply to a schoolteacher who criticized*
> *him for using the word "ain't"*

BOB UECKER

A National League catcher whose acting and broadcasting careers far over-shadowed his time spent on the field.

I knew when my career was over. In 1965 my baseball card came out with no picture.

I signed with the Milwaukee Braves for three thousand dollars. That bothered my dad at the time because he didn't have that kind of dough. But he eventually scraped it up.

They said I was such a great prospect that they were sending me to a winter league to sharpen up. When I stepped off the plane, I was in Greenland.

The highlight of my career? In '67 with St. Louis, I walked with the bases loaded to drive in the winning run in an intersquad game in spring training.

Baseball

They've got so many Latin players we're going to have to get a Latin instructor up here.

—*Phil Rizzuto*

Age is a case of mind over matter. If you don't mind, it don't matter.

—*Satchel Paige*

I heard the doctors revived a man after being dead for four-and-a-half minutes. When they asked what it was like being dead, he said it was like listening to New York Yankees announcer Phil Rizzuto during a rain delay.

—Late Night *host David Letterman*

Strangely, in slow motion replay, the ball seemed to hang in the air for even longer.

—*David Acfield, sports commentator*

During the 1957 World Series, Yankee catcher Yogi Berra noticed that the Atlanta Braves hitting star Hank Aaron grasped the bat the wrong way. "Turn it around," he said, "so you can see the trademark." Aaron kept his eye on the pitcher's mound: "Didn't come up here to read. Came up here to hit."

When we played, World Series checks meant something. Now all they do is screw your taxes.

—*Don Drysdale*

I hated to bat against (Don) Drysdale. After he hit you he'd come around, look at the bruise on your arm and say, "Do you want me to sign it?"

—*Mickey Mantle*

If you hit Polonia 100 fly balls, you could make a movie out of it— Catch 22.

—*pitcher Dennis Lamp on outfielder Luis Polonia's defensive abilities*

When we played softball, I'd steal second base, feel guilty and go back.

— *Woody Allen*

For the parents of a Little Leaguer, a baseball game is simply a nervous breakdown into innings.

—Earl Wilson

I made a game effort to argue but two things were against me: the umpires and the rules.

—Giants manager Leo Durocher

If he raced his pregnant wife, he'd finish third.

—Tommy LaSorda on catcher Mike Scioscia

Soccer

I took a whack on my left ankle, but something told me it was my right.

—*Lee Hendrie*

I couldn't settle in Italy—it was like living in a foreign country.

—*Ian Rush*

Interviewer: "Would it be fair to describe you as a volatile player?"

David Beckham: "Well, I can play in the centre, on the right and occasionally on the left side."

I always used to put my right boot on first, and then obviously my
right sock.

—*Barry Venison*

The Brazilians were South America, and the Ukranians will be
more European.

—*Phil Neville*

All that remains is for a few dots and commas to be crossed.

—*Mitchell Thomas*

One accusation you can't throw at me is that I've always done my best.

—*Alan Shearer*

I'd rather play in front of a full house than an empty crowd.

—*Johnny Giles*

I would not be bothered if we lost every game as long as we won the league.

—*Mark Viduka*

He's put on weight and I've lost it, and vice versa.

—Ronnie Whelan

If you don't believe you can win, there is no point in getting out of bed at the end of the day.

—Neville Southall

We lost because we didn't win.

—Ronaldo

Well, Clive, it's all about the two M's—movement and positioning.

—*Ron Atkinson*

I've had 14 bookings this season—8 of which were my fault, but 7 of which were disputable.

—*Paul Gascoigne*

I've never wanted to leave. I'm here for the rest of my life, and hopefully after that as well.

—*Alan Shearer*

I'd like to play for an Italian club, like Barcelona.

—*Mark Draper*

Without being too harsh on David Beckham, he cost us the match.

—*Ian Wright*

I'm as happy as I can be—but I have been happier.

—*Ugo Ehiogu*

Leeds is a great club and it's been my home for years, even though I live in Middlesbrough.

—*Jonathan Woodgate*

I can see the carrot at the end of the tunnel.

—*Stuart Pearce*

I was surprised, but I always say nothing surprises me in football.

—*Les Ferdinand*

There's no in between—you're either good or bad. We were
in between.

—*Gary Lineker*

Winning doesn't really matter as long as you win.

—*Vinny Jones*

English football commentators

He's 31 this year: last year he was 30.

—*David Coleman*

The ageless Dennis Wise, now in his thirties.

—*Martin Tyler*

The Italians are hoping for an Italian victory.

—*David Coleman*

Ian Rush is deadly 10 times out of 10, but that wasn't one of them.
—*Peter Jones*

Martin O'Neill, standing, hands on hips, stroking his chin.
—*Mike Ingham*

Such a positive move by Uruguay—bringing 2 players off and putting 2 players on.
—*John Helm*

It's now 1–1, an exact reversal of the scoreline on Saturday.

—*Radio 5 Live*

You don't score 64 goals in 86 games without being able to score goals.

—*Alan Green*

Celtic manager Davic Hay still has a fresh pair of legs up his sleeve

—*John Greig*

And with just 4 minutes gone, the score is already 0–0.

—Ian Darke

Good evening. The game you are about to see is the most stupid, appalling, disgusting and disgraceful exhibition of football, possibly in the history of the game.

—David Coleman

The USA are a goal down, and if they don't get a goal they'll lose.

—John Helm

Lukic saved with his foot, which is all part of the goalkeeper's arm.

—*Barry Davies*

Sporting Lisbon in their green and white hoops, looking like a team of zebras.

—*Peter Jones*

If that had gone in, it would have been a goal.

—*David Coleman*

The lad got over-excited when he saw the whites of the goalpost's eyes.

—*Steve Coppell*

For those of you watching in black and white, Spurs are in the all-yellow strip.

—*John Motson*

With news of Scotland's 0–0 victory over Holland . . .

—*Scottish television announcer*

Football

Football is a mistake. It combines two of the worst things about American life. It is violence punctuated by committee meetings.

—George F. Will

I want to rush for 1,000 or 1,500 yards, whichever comes first.

—Runningback George Rogers, about the upcoming season

See the New York Jets play the Cinncinnati Bagels this Sunday on NBC.

—unidentified TV announcer

I have two weapons: my arms, my legs and my brains.
—*Michael Vick, Atlanta Falcons quarterback*

One player was lost because he broke his nose. How do you go about getting a nose in condition for football?
—*Darrell Royal, Texas football coach, on Longhorn injuries resulting from poor physical conditioning*

If only faces could talk . . .
—*Pat Summerall, sportscaster, during the Super Bowl*

The Rose Bowl is the only bowl I've ever seen that I didn't have to clean.

—*Erma Bombeck*

An atheist is a guy who watches a Notre Dame-SMU football game and doesn't care who wins.

—*Dwight D. Eisenhower*

He treats us like men. He lets us wear earrings.

—*Torrin Polk, University of Houston receiver, on his coach, John Jenkins*

Are you any relation to your brother, Marv?

—Leon Wood, New Jersey Nets guard,
to Steve Albert, Nets TV commentator

The reason women don't play football is because eleven of them would never wear the same outfit in public.

—Phyllis Diller

Nobody in football should be called a genius. A genius is a guy like Norman Einstein.

—Joe Theismann

Golf

Golf is a good walk spoiled.

—*Mark Twain*

Golf is a game whose aim is to hit a very small ball into an even smaller hole, with weapons singularly ill-designed for the purpose.

—*Winston Churchill*

I had a wonderful experience on the golf course today. I had a hole in nothing. Missed the ball and sank the divot.

—*Don Adams*

I have a tip that can take five strokes off anyone's golf game. It's called an eraser.

—*Arnold Palmer*

Columbus went around the world in 1492. That isn't a lot of strokes when you consider the course.

—*Lee Trevino*

Although golf was originally restricted to wealthy, overweight Protestants, today it's open to anybody who owns hideous clothing.

—*Dave Barry*

Middle age occurs when you are too young to take up golf and too old to rush up to the net.

—*Franklin P. Adams*

He has a wonderful short game . . . unfortunately it is off the tee.

—*Jimmy Demaret on Bob Hope's golf game*

The least thing upset him on the links. He missed short putts because of the uproar of the butterflies in the adjoining meadows.

—*P. G. Wodehouse*

If you're caught on a golf course during a storm and are afraid of lightning, hold up a 1-iron. Not even God can hit a 1-iron.

—*Lee Trevino*

I've had a good day when I don't fall out of the cart.

—*Buddy Hackett*

I know I am getting better at golf because I am hitting fewer spectators.

—*Gerald Ford*

Golf appeals to the idiot in us and the child. Just how childlike
golf players become is proven by their frequent inability to count
past five.

—*John Updike*

It took me seventeen years to get three thousand hits in baseball.
I did it in one afternoon on the golf course.

—*Hank Aaron*

The Supreme Court ruled that disabled golfer Casey Martin has a
legal right to ride in a golf cart between shots at PGA Tour events.
Man, the next thing you know, they're going to have some guy carry
his clubs around for him.

—*Jon Stewart*

If I were you, I'd lay off for a couple of weeks . . . and then quit.
—*Jimmy Demaret on Johnny Carson's golf swing*

The other day I broke 70. That's a lot of clubs.
—*Henny Youngman*

I'm not saying my golf game went bad, but if I grew tomatoes, they'd come up sliced.
—*Lee Trevino*

The people who gave us golf and called it a game are the same people who gave us bagpipes and called it music.

—*source unknown*

After all these years, it's still embarrassing for me to play on the American golf tour. Like the time I asked my caddie for a sand wedge, and he came back ten minutes later with a ham on rye.

—*Chi Chi Rodriguez*

Boxing

Sure there have been injuries and deaths in boxing—but none of them serious.

—*Alan Minter*

It pays me better to knock teeth out than to put them in.
                                        —*Frank Moran, dentist turned prizefighter, when Theodore Roosevelt asked him why he changed occupations*

[Joe] Frazier is so ugly that he should donate his face to the U.S. Bureau of Wildlife.

—*Muhammad Ali*

I don't like money, actually, but it quiets my nerves.

—*Joe Louis*

"Superman don't need no seat belt," Muhammud Ali once told a flight attendant, who replied, "Superman doesn't need no airplane either." Ali fastened the belt.

Introduced to Ali, violinist Isaac Stern said, "You might say we're in the same business—we both earn a living with our hands."
"You must be pretty good," said Ali. "There isn't a mark on you."

They're selling video cassettes of the Ali-Spinks fight for $89.95. Hell, for that money, Spinks will come to your house.

—*Ferdie Pacheco*

I fought Sugar [Ray Robinson] so many times, I'm surprised I'm not diabetic. But I did have him off the canvas once . . . when he stepped over my body to leave the ring.

—*Jake LaMotta*

He's a guy who gets up at six o'clock in the morning regardless of what time it is.

—*Lou Duva, veteran boxing trainer*

I'm so fast that last night I turned off the light switch in my hotel room and was in bed before the room was dark.

—*Muhammud Ali*

Tennis

The serve was invented so that the net could play.

—Bill Cosby

These ball boys are marvelous. You don't even notice them. There's a left-handed one over there. I noticed him earlier.

—Max Robertson

It's quite clear that Virginia Wade is thriving on the pressure now that the pressure on her to do well is off.

—Harry Carpenter

When Martina is tense, it helps her relax.

—*Dan Maskell*

Strawberries, cream and champers flowed like hot cakes.

—*BBC Radio 2*

She comes from a tennis playing family. Her father's a dentist.

—*BBC 2*

We haven't had any more rain since it stopped raining.

—*Harry Carpenter*

Horse Racing

I played a great horse yesterday—it took seven horses to beat him.

—Henny Youngman

They must get to the end and go, "We were just here." What's the point of that?

—Jerry Seinfeld, on what a horse must think after a race is over

I hope I break even—I need the money.

—Joe E. Lewis

The horse I bet on was so slow, the jockey kept a diary of the trip.
—*Henny Youngman*

A man described as a "sportsman" is generally a bookmaker who takes actresses to nightclubs.
—*Jimmy Cannon*

The race is not always to the swift, nor the battle to the strong, but that's the way to bet.
—*Damon Runyon*

I bet on a horse that went off at ten to one. He finished at two-thirty.
—*Henny Youngman*

Basketball

Nothing there but basketball, a game which won't be fit for people until they set the basket umbilicus-high and return the giraffes to the zoo.

—*Ogden Nash*

Part of the charm of basketball lies in the fact that it's a simple game to understand. Players race up and down a fairly small area indoors and stuff the ball into a ring with Madonna's dress hanging on it.

—*Dan Jenkins*

The trouble with referees is that they just don't care which side wins.

—*Tom Canterbury*

Chemistry is a class you take in high school or college, where you figure out two plus two is ten, or something.

—*Dennis Rodman*

We all get heavier as we get older because there's a lot more information in our heads.

—*Vlade Divac, basketball player*

And the rest

I can't see who's in the lead, but it's either Oxford or Cambridge.
>   —John Snagg, announcing the
>   Oxford-Cambridge boat race

With half of the race gone, there is half of the race still to go.
>   —motorsports commentator Murray Walker

What I said to them at half time would be unprintable on the radio.
>   —Gerry Francis

I was in Saint-Etienne two years ago. It's much the same as it is now, although now it's completely different.

—*Kevin Keegan, BBC*

Mansell is gazing at him through his microphone.

—*Murray Walker*

It's a great advantage to be able to hurdle with both legs.

—*BBC sports commentator David Coleman*

Owen runs like rabbit chasing after what do rabbits run after? They run after nothing. Well, running after other rabbits.

—*track and field announcer Tom Tyrell*

And for the
non-sporting breed . . .

Sport—I never, ever got involved in sport.
—Winston Churchill on the secret of his longevity

I get my exercise acting as a pallbearer to my friends who exercise.
—Chauncey Depew

The first time I see a jogger smiling, I'll consider it.
—Joan Rivers

Jogging is for people who aren't intelligent enough to
watch television.

—Victoria Wood

I don't jog. If I die I want to be sick.

—Abe Lemons, U.S. basketball coach

The only reason I would take up jogging is so I could hear heavy
breathing again.

—Erma Bombeck

III.

SHOW BIZ ANTICS

Give the Public What They Want

It proves what they always say: give the public what they want and they'll come out for it.

—Red Skelton, on the funeral of Harry Cohn,
a widely disliked movie producer

Then there was the blonde actress who was so dumb, she slept with the screenwriter.

—source unknown

I'm an excellent housekeeper. Every time I get a divorce, I keep the house.

—Zsa Zsa Gabor

In Hollywood, if you don't have happiness you send out for it.

—*Rex Reed*

Give me a couple of years, and I'll make that actress an overnight success.

—*Samuel Goldwyn*

I only put clothes on so that I'm not naked when I go out shopping.

—*Julia Roberts*

Every night, I have to read a book, so that my mind will stop
thinking about things that I stress about.

—*Britney Spears*

I think most people are curious about what it would be like to be able
to meet yourself—it's eerie.

—*Christie Turlington*

I'm so naive about finances. Once when my mother mentioned
an amount and I realized I didn't understand, she had to explain:
"That's like three Mercedes." Then I understood.

—*Brooke Shields*

So, where's the Cannes Film Festival being held this year?

—*Christina Aguilera*

On the one hand, [men] will never experience childbirth. On the other hand, we can open all our own jars.

—*Bruce Willis*

A gentleman is simply a patient wolf.

—*Lana Turner*

They used to shoot [Shirley Temple] through gauze. You should shoot me through linoleum.

—*Tallulah Bankhead*

When an actor comes to me and wants to discuss his character, I say, "It's in the script." If he says, "But what's my motivation?" I say, "Your salary."

—*Alfred Hitchcock*

Do you think we should drive a stake through his heart just in case?
—*Peter Lorre to Vincent Price at Bela Lugosi's funeral*

You know you're getting old when everything hurts. And what doesn't hurt doesn't work.

—*Ily Gardner*

What do you want me to do? Stop shooting now and release it as *The Five Commandments*?

—*Cecil B. DeMille, after running over budget on the filming of* The Ten Commandments

I did a picture in England one winter and it was so cold, I almost got married.

—*Shelley Winters*

In Hollywood a marriage is a success if it outlasts milk.

—*Rita Rudner*

Joan always cries a lot. Her tear ducts must be close to her bladder.

—*Bette Davis on Joan Crawford*

She ought to be arrested for loitering in front of an orchestra.

—*Bette Midler on Helen Reddy*

As well-endowed actress Jayne Mansfield bent over at a Hollywood reception, one of her ample breasts tumbled out of her dress. "Please, Miss Mansfield," Clifton Webb told her, "we're wine drinkers at this table."

Alfred Hitchcock was once detained by an airport customs officer who studied the director's passport's listing his occupation as "Producer." "So what do you produce?" the official asked.

"Gooseflesh!" Hitchcock replied.

Fame means when your computer modem is broken, the repair guy comes out to your house a little faster.

—*Sandra Bullock*

Hollywood is a place where they place you under contract instead of under observation.

—*Walter Winchell*

To survive there [Hollywood], you need the ambition of a Latin-American revolutionary, the ego of a grand opera tenor, and the physical stamina of a cow pony.

—*Billie Burke*

You can pick out actors by the glazed look that comes into their eyes when the conversation wanders away from themselves.

—*Michael Wilding*

I stopped believing in Santa Claus when I was six. Mother took me to see him in a department store and he asked for my autograph.

—*Shirley Temple*

For those of you haven't read the book, it's being published tomorrow.

—*David Frost*

Clark is the sort of guy that if you say, "Hiya, Clark, how are you?" he's stuck for an answer.

—*Ava Gardner on Clark Gable*

"Mr. Barrymore, I am never going to act with you again."

John Barrymore: "My dear, you still haven't."

> —*Katharine Hepburn after making the film* A Bill of Divorcement

The scene is dull. Tell him to put more life into his dying.
> —*Samuel Goldwyn*

Bruse Baldwin: "He's got a lot of charm."

Hildy Johnson: "Well, he comes by it naturally. His grandfather was a snake."

> —*from* His Girl Friday, *screenplay by Charles Lederer*

During a rehearsal one day, Elaine Stritch began to sing, "When the tower of Babel fell," and pronounced the line to rhyme with "scrabble."

Noel Coward promptly corrected her: "It's 'baybel.'"

"I've always said 'babble,'" the actress replied. "Everyone says 'babble.' It means mixed-up language, doesn't it? Gibberish. That's where we get the word 'babble' from."

"No," replied Coward. "That's a fabble."

It's one of the tragic ironies of the theatre that only one man in it can count on steady work—the night watchman.

—*Tallulah Bankhead*

It's a scientific fact. For every year a person lives in Hollywood, they lose two points of their IQ.

—*Truman Capote*

He's the type of man who will end up dying in his own arms.

—*Mamie Van Doren on Warren Beatty*

I once shook hands with Pat Boone and my whole right side sobered up.

—*Dean Martin*

There are good days and there are bad days, and this is one of them.

—*Lawrence Welk*

He [Harry Belafonte] was wearing a velvet shirt open to the navel. And he didn't have one. Which is either a show business gimmick, or the ultimate rejection of mother.

—*Mort Sahl*

Man, I am a one-eyed, black Jew! That's my handicap!

—*Sammy Davis, Jr., asked about his golf handicap*

I knew her before she was a virgin.

—Oscar Levant, on Doris Day

Smoking kills. If you're killed, you've lost a very important part of your life.

—Brooke Shields

Every director bites the hand that lays the golden egg.

—Samuel Goldwyn

Cesar Romero would attend the opening of a napkin.

—*Jim Backus*

An actor's success has the life expectancy of a small boy about to look into a gas tank with a lighted match.

—*Fred Allen*

If people don't want to go to the picture, nobody can stop them.

—*Samuel Goldwyn*

I've been doing the Fonda workout: the Peter Fonda workout. That's where I wake up, take a hit of acid, smoke a joint, and run to my sister's house and ask her for money.

—*Kevin Meaney*

In fifty years, he never worked a day. To him, nine to five was odds on a horse.

—*Archie Bunker*, All in the Family

She has discovered the secret of perpetual middle age.

—*Oscar Levant on Zsa Zsa Gabor*

You can calculate Zsa Zsa Gabor's age by the rings on her fingers.
—*Bob Hope*

Zsa Zsa Gabor has been married so many times she has rice marks on her face.
—*Henny Youngman*

She ran the whole gamut of emotions from A to B.
—*Dorothy Parker on Katharine Hepburn*

Elizabeth Taylor's so fat, she puts mayonnaise on aspirin.

—*Joan Rivers*

Her hair lounges on her shoulders like an anesthetized cocker spaniel.

—*Henry Allen on Lauren Bacall*

Each generation has been an education for us in different ways. The first child-with-bloody-nose was rushed to the emergency room. The fifth child-with-bloody-nose was told to go to the yard immediately and stop bleeding on the carpet.

—*Art Linkletter*

If it's not the sheriff, it's the finance company. I've got more attachments on me than a vacuum cleaner.

—John Barrymore

I don't see what the big deal is about same-sex marriages. Every married couple I know has the same sex all the time.

—Jim Rosenberg

Many a man has fallen in love with a girl in a light so dim he would not have chosen a suit by it.

—Maurice Chevalier

The perfect lover is one who turns into a pizza at 4:00 A.M.

—*Charles Pierce*

I never mind my wife having the last word. In fact, I'm delighted when she gets to it.

—*Walter Matthau*

He couldn't ad-lib a fart after a baked-bean dinner.

—*Johnny Carson on Chevy Chase*

She speaks five languages and can't act in any of them.

—John Gielgud on Ingrid Bergman

Joan Collins unfortunately can't be with us tonight. She's busy attending the birth of her next husband.

—John Parrott

She turned down the role of Helen Keller because she couldn't remember the lines.

—Joan Rivers on Bo Derek

Maybe it's the hair. Maybe it's the teeth. Maybe it's the intellect. No, it's the hair.

—*Tom Shales on Farrah Fawcett*

The closest thing to Roseanne Barr's singing the national anthem was my cat being neutered.

—*Johnny Carson*

I want them to play Britney Spears at my funeral. That way I won't feel so bad about being dead, and everyone there will know there is something worse than death.

—*Gary Numan*

A verbal contract isn't worth the paper it's written on.

—*Samuel Goldwyn*

I could eat alphabet soup and shit better lyrics.

—Johnny Mercer about a British musical

A studio usher knocked on the door of venerable actress Ethel Barry-more's dressing room. "A couple of gals in the reception room, Miss Barrymore, who say they went to school with you. What shall I do?"

"Wheel them in," Ms. Barrymore replied.

All through the five acts of that Shakespearean tragedy, he played the king as though under a momentary apprehension that someone else was about to play the ace.

—Eugene Field reviewing a performance of King Lear

On a television program during which celebrities sought miscella-neous guidance from a group of panelists that included the noted wit George S. Kaufman, singer Eddie Fisher asked about a young woman who refused to go out with him on account of his advancing age.

"Mr. Fisher," Kaufman advised, "on Mount Wilson there is a telescope that can magnify the most distant stars up to twenty-four times the magnification of any previous telescope. This remarkable instrument was unsurpassed in the world of astronomy until the development and construction of the Mount Palomar telescope—an even more remarkable instrument of magnification. Owing to advances and improvements in optical technology, it is capable of magnifying the stars to four times the magnification and resolution of the Mount Wilson telescope."

"Mr. Fisher," Kaufman continued, "if you could somehow put the Mount Wilson telescope inside the Mount Palomar telescope, you still wouldn't be able to detect my interest in your problem."

"Hello, Arthur. This is your mother. Do you remember me? . . . Someday you'll get married and have children of your own and Honey, when you do, I only pray that they'll make you suffer the way you're making me. That's a Mother's Prayer."

—*Mike Nichols and Elaine May comedy routine*

Transported to a surreal landscape, a young girl kills the first woman she meets and then teams up with three complete strangers to kill again.

—*Marin County (California) newspaper's*
TV listing for The Wizard of Oz

Actor Dustin Farnum: "I've never been better! In the last act yesterday, I had the audience glued to their seats."

Oliver Herford: "How clever of you to think of it."

FROM *THE SIMPSONS*

This long-running sitcom is also the longest-running animated show in TV history. Bumbling paterfamilias Homer Simpson stands out as one of America's cultural icons.

Dealer: "19."

Homer: "Hit me!"

Dealer: "20."

Homer: "Hit me!"

Dealer: "21."

Homer: "Hit me!"

Dealer: "22."

Homer: "D'oh!"

Mulder: "All right, Homer. We want you to re-create your every move the night you saw this alien."

Homer: "Well, the evening began at the gentleman's club, where we were discussing Wittgenstein over a game of backgammon."

Scully: "Mr. Simpson, it's a felony to lie to the F.B.I."

Homer: "We were sitting in Barney's car eating packets of mustard. You happy now?"

Homer: "Weaseling out of things is important to learn. It's what separates us from the animals . . . except the weasel."

Barney: "I'm Barney Gumble, and I'm an alcoholic."

Lisa: "Mr. Gumble, this is a Girl Scout meeting."

Barney: "Is it? Or is it that you girls can't admit that you have a problem!"

FROM *CHEERS*

This popular TV sitcom was set in a Boston bar. Patron Norm's affection for beer was a recurring theme.

Sam (the bartender): "What'll you have, Normie?"

Norm: "Well, I'm in a gambling mood, Sammy. I'll take a glass of whatever comes out of that tap."

Sam: "Looks like beer, Norm."

Norm: "Call me Mister Lucky."

Woody (the bartender): "What's the story, Mr. Peterson?"

Norm: "The Bobbsey Twins Go to the Brewery. Let's cut to the happy ending."

Woody: How would a beer feel, Mr. Peterson?

Norm: Pretty nervous if I was in the room.

Coach (another bartender): What would you say to a beer, Normie?

Norm: Daddy wuvs you.

IV

POLITICAL BADINAGE

Catapult the Propaganda

GEORGE W. BUSH

B
U
S
H

The forty-third president of the United States, Bush is the frequent source of puzzlement and amusement over his use and misuse of the language.

See, in my line of work you got to keep repeating things over and over and over again for the truth to sink in, to kind of catapult the propaganda.

Oftentimes, we live in a processed world, you know, people focus on the process and not results.

It will take time to restore chaos and order.

They have miscalculated me as a leader.

I am mindful not only of preserving executive powers for myself, but for predecessors as well.

I strongly believe what we're doing is the right thing. If I didn't believe it—I'm going to repeat what I said before—I'd pull the troops out, nor if I believed we could win, I would pull the troops out.

No question that the enemy has tried to spread sectarian violence. They use violence as a tool to do that.

If the Iranians were to have a nuclear weapon, they could proliferate.

And so I'm for medical liability at the federal level.

B

U

S

H

Because he's hiding.

> *—responding to a reporter who asked why*
> *Osama bin Laden had not been caught*

Natural gas is hemispheric. I like to call it hemispheric in nature because it is a product that we can find in our neighborhoods.

They misunderestimated me.

If you don't stand for anything, you don't stand for anything! If you don't stand for something, you don't stand for anything.

We cannot let terrorists and rogue nations hold this nation hostile or hold our allies hostile.

DAN QUAYLE

Vice-president under George H. W. Bush, Quayle set the standard for political malapropisms and obfuscation.

Republicans understand the importance of bondage between a mother and child.

One word sums up probably the responsibility of any vice president, and that one word is "to be prepared."

Welcome to President Bush, Mrs. Bush, and my fellow astronauts.

Q
U
A
Y
L
E

QUAYLE

Mars is essentially in the same orbit. . . . Mars is somewhat the same distance from the Sun, which is very important. We have seen pictures where there are canals, we believe, and water. If there is water, that means there is oxygen. If oxygen, that means we can breathe.

The Holocaust was an obscene period in our nation's history. I mean in this century's history. But we all lived in this century. I didn't live in this century.

I believe we are on an irreversible trend toward more freedom and democracy—but that could change.

I have made good judgments in the past. I have made good judgments in the future.

The future will be better tomorrow.

We're going to have the best-educated American people in the world.

People that are really very weird can get into sensitive positions and have a tremendous impact on history.

We have a firm commitment to NATO, we are a part of NATO.
We have a firm commitment to Europe. We are a part of Europe.

I am not part of the problem. I am a Republican.

I love California. I practically grew up in Phoenix.

RONALD REAGAN

The fortieth U.S. president, Reagan made good use of his acting background to use humor as a valuable tool.

The taxpayer—that's someone who works for the federal government but doesn't have to take the civil service examination.

I don't know. I've never played a governor.
> —*asked by a reporter in 1966 what kind of governor he would be*

Facts are stupid things.
> —*at the 1988 Republican National Convention, attempting to quote John Adams, who said, "Facts are stubborn things."*

Trees cause more pollution than automobiles.

All the waste in a year from a nuclear power plant can be stored under a desk.

They say hard work never hurt anybody, but I figure why take the chance.

Approximately 80 percent of our air pollution stems from hydrocarbons released by vegetation, so let's not go overboard in setting and enforcing tough emission standards from man-made sources.

Recession is when your neighbor loses his job. Depression is when you lose yours. And recovery is when Jimmy Carter loses his.

R

E

A

G

A

N

How are you, Mr. Mayor? I'm glad to meet you. How are things in
your city?
>   —*greeting Samual Pierce, his secretary of Housing and Urban*
>   *Development, during a White House reception for mayors*

What makes him think a middle-aged actor, who's played with a
chimp, could have a future in politics?
>   —*on Clint Eastwood's bid to*
>   *become mayor of Carmel.*

There were four million people in the Colonies and we had Jefferson
and Franklin. Now we have over 200 million and the two top guys
are Clinton and Dole. What can you draw from this? Darwin
was wrong!

—*Mort Sahl*

Reader, suppose you were an idiot; and suppose you were a member
of Congress; but I repeat myself.

— *Mark Twain*

I would go to the President's wife and apologize, and then leave
at once.

—*Maine Senator Margaret Chase Smith, asked what she would do
if she woke up one morning and found herself in the White House.*

The meek shall inherit the earth, but not the mineral rights.

—*J. Paul Getty*

The one thing I do not want to be called is First Lady. It sounds like a saddle horse.

—*Jacqueline Kennedy*

The puppies are sleeping on the *Washington Post* and *The New York Times*. It's the first time in history these papers have been used to *prevent* leaks.

—*George H.W. Bush*

If life were fair, Dan Quayle would be making a living asking,
"Do you want fries with that?"

— *John Cleese*

This is really embarrassing. I just forgot our state governor's name,
but I know that you will help me recall him.

—*Arnold Schwarzenegger*

Things are more like today than they have ever been before.

—*Gerald R. Ford*

People are more violently opposed to fur than leather because it's safer to harass rich women than motorcycle gangs.

—*source unknown*

I have opinions of my own, strong opinions, but I don't always agree with them.

—*George H. W. Bush*

What's a man got to do to get in the top fifty?
                —*Bill Clinton, reacting to a survey of journalists*
                that ranked the Lewinsky scandal as the fifty-third
                most significant story of the century

I have often wanted to drown my troubles, but I can't get my wife to go swimming.

—*Jimmy Carter*

I was provided with additional input that was radically different from the truth. I assisted in furthering that version.

—*Colonel Oliver North, from his Iran-Contra testimony*

I think that gay marriage should be between a man and a woman.

—*Arnold Schwarzenegger*

In Arizona we have so little water that the trees chase the dogs.
—*Senator Barry Goldwater*

Confronted at a White House reception by a large, obviously self-satisfied Beacon Hill matron, Coolidge allowed his visitor to pump his arm mechanically while she gushed, "Oh, Mr. President, I'm from Boston." "Yep," he shot back. "And you'll never get over it."

Harry Truman's daughter Margaret brought home (which is to say, to the White House) a young man in whom she was most interested. After the introductions and a time of somewhat awkward, halting conversation, the president tried to put the young man at ease by asking if he would like to see his prize roses.

The president, his daughter and the young man exited to the rose garden. As they walked among the plants, the young man asked the president the secret of his success with roses. "Manure," replied the president, "and lots of it," going on at some length about the proper kind of fertilizer.

After about five minutes of such talk, a mortified Margaret ran to her mother in tears, pleading, "You must stop Father from talking about manure—it is very embarrassing."

Bess Truman replied, "I'll see what I can do, dear, but you have no idea how many years it has taken me to get your father to call it 'manure.'"

—various sources

Nixon is the kind of politician who would cut down a redwood tree, then mount the stump for a speech on conservation.

—*Adlai Stevenson*

If a politician found he had cannibals among his constituents, he would promise them missionaries for dinner.

—*H. L. Mencken*

The difference between a misfortune and a calamity is this: If Gladstone fell into the Thames, it would be a misfortune. But if someone dragged him out again, that would be a calamity.

—*Benjamin Disraeli*

At every crisis the Kaiser crumpled. In defeat he fled; in revolution he abdicated; in exile he remarried.

> —*Winston Churchill*

There but for the grace of God—goes God.

> —*Winston Churchill, on Stafford Cripps*

Churchill's critics called him a rash, impetuous, tactless, contentious, inconsistent, unsound, and amusing parliamentary celebrity who was forever out of step. "We just don't know what to make of him," a troubled Conservative Member of Parliament told Lady Astor.

She paused and then smiled, "How about a nice rug?"

When planning what to wear to a costume ball Lady Astor was hosting, Churchill asked her for suggestions.

Her reply: "Why don't you come sober, Mr. Prime Minister."

Lady Astor once said with exasperation to Churchill, "If you were my husband, I'd put arsenic in your coffee."

Churchill responded, "Madam, if I were your husband, I'd drink it."

He has devoted the best years of his life to preparing his impromptu speeches.

> —*Earl of Birkenhead on Sir Winston Churchill*

He would kill his own mother just so that he could use her skin to make a drum to beat his own praises.

— Margot Asquith on Sir Winston Churchill

He has all the virtues I dislike and none of the vices I admire.

—attributed to Sir Winston Churchill

Lady Astor to Winston Churchill: "Sir, you're drunk!"

Churchill's reply: "Yes, madam, and you're ugly. But in the morning, I will be sober and you will still be ugly."

When your back's against the wall it's time to turn round and fight.

—*John Major*

I got a letter from the IRS. Apparently I owe them $800. So I sent them a letter back. I said, "If you'll remember, I fastened my return with a paper clip, which according to your very own latest government Pentagon spending figures will more than make up for the difference."

—*Emo Philips*

Congressman John Randolf and Henry Clay met on a sidewalk in Washington.

Clay: "I, sir, do not step aside for a scoundrel."

Randolf: "On the other hand, I always do."

When Lord Sandwich offered the opinion that John Wilkes,
an eighteenth-century British journalist and politician would die
"either of the pox or on the gallows," Wilkes shot back, "That
will depend on whether I embrace your lordship's mistress or your
lordship's principles."

The private enterprise system indicates that some people have higher
incomes than others.

> —*Former Governor Jerry Brown of California*

I've read about foreign policy and studied—I know the number
of continents.

> —*George Wallace, 1968 presidential campaign*

I watch a lot of baseball on the radio.

—*Gerald R. Ford*

I can't think of any existing law that's in force that wasn't before.

—*George H. W. Bush*

Your food stamps will be stopped effective March 1992 because we received notice that you passed away. May God bless you. You may reapply if there is a change in your circumstances.

—*Department of Social Services,*
Greenville, South Carolina

Whenever a Republican leaves one side of the aisle and goes to the other, it raises the intelligence quotient of both parties.

> —*Republican Senator Claire Booth Luce, commenting on a certain Republican senator's becoming a Democrat*

When John F. Kennedy was on the presidential campaign trail in West Virginia, a coal miner challenged him with, "Is it true that you haven't done an honest day of hard labor in your life?" Kennedy was obliged to admit that was correct and waited for further chastisement. But the miner shook his hand and replied, "Believe me, you haven't missed a thing."

Clement Atlee said that Herbert Morrison was his own worst enemy. To which Ernest Bevin replied, "Not while I'm alive he ain't."

American politicians will do anything for money; English politicians will take the money and won't do anything.

—*Stephen Leacock*

Q: How do you tell Al Gore from the Secret Service Agents?

A: He's the stiff one.

—*source unknown*

Nixon's motto was: If two wrongs don't make a right, try three.

—*Norman Cousins*

Politicians and diapers have one thing in common. They should both be changed regularly . . . and for the same reason.

—*source unknown*

Those who survived the San Francisco earthquake said, "Thank God, I'm still alive." But, of course, those who died, their lives will never be the same again.

—*Senator Barbara Boxer, (D, Calif.)*

Joey Bishop (talk-show host): "Would you like to become a regular on the show?"

Barry Goldwater: "No, thank you. I'd much rather watch you in bed with my wife."

You know, if I were a single man, I might ask that mummy out. That's a good-looking mummy!
>   —*Bill Clinton, looking at the Inca mummy "Juanita"*

For those of you who don't understand Reaganomics, it's based on the principle that the rich and the poor will get the same amount of ice. In Reaganomics, however, the poor get all of theirs in winter.
>   —*Morris Udall*

You can't just let nature run wild.
>   —*Walter Hickel, former governor of Alaska*

The difference between death and taxes is death doesn't get worse every time Congress meets.

Will Rogers

Politics gives guys so much power that they tend to behave badly around women. And I hope I never get into that.

—*Bill Clinton*

I do not like this word "bomb." It is not a bomb. It is a device that is exploding.

—*Jacques le Blanc, French ambassador on nuclear weapons*

I think with a lifetime appointment to the Supreme Court, you can't play, you know, hide the salami, or whatever it's called.
    —*Democratic Party Chairman Howard Dean, urging President Bush to make public Supreme Court nominee Harriet Miers's White House records, October 5, 2005*

I am not going to give you a number for it because it's not my business to do intelligent work.
    —*Defense Secretary Donald Rumsfeld, asked to estimate the number of Iraqi insurgents while testifying before Congress, February 16, 2005*

He knows nothing and thinks he knows everything. That points clearly to a political career.

— *George Bernard Shaw*

They never open their mouths without subtracting from the sum of human knowledge.

— *Speaker of the House Thomas Reed of two fellow congressmen*

The Democrats are the party that says government will make you smarter, taller, richer, and remove the crabgrass on your lawn. The Republicans are the party that says government doesn't work and then they get elected and prove it.

— *P. J. O'Rourke*

The Democrats seem to be basically nicer people, but they have demonstrated time and again that they have the management skills of celery.

—*Dave Barry*

When Al Gore gives a fireside chat, the fire goes out.

—*Bob Dole*

The word *liberty* in the mouth of Mr. Webster sounds like the word *love* in the mouth of a courtesan.

—*Ralph Waldo Emerson*

He's the only man able to walk under a bed without hitting his head.
  —*Walter Winchell on presidential candidate Thomas E. Dewey*

He no play-a the game, he no make-a the rules.
  —*Secretary of Agriculture Earl Butz on Pope Pius XII's attitude toward birth control*

Don't be so humble, you're not that great.
  —*Golda Meir to Moshe Dayan*

That scoundrel deserves to be kicked to death by a jackass, and I'm just the one to do it.

—*A congressional candidate in Texas*

A billion here, a billion there, sooner or later it adds up to real money.

—*Everett Dirksen, Congressman*

Solutions are not the answer.

—*Richard Nixon*

The Right Honourable Gentleman is indebted to his memory for his jests and to his imagination for his facts.
—Richard Brinsley Sheridan on the Earl of Dundas

She was happy as the dey was long.
—Lord Norbury on Queen Caroline's
affair with the Dey of Algiers

His intellect is of no more use than a pistol packed in the bottom of a trunk in the robber infested Apennines.
—Prince Albert on his son Edward, Prince of Wales,
later King Edward VII

Oh, if I could piss the way he speaks!
—*Georges Clemenceau on David Lloyd George*

Attila the Hen.
—*Clement Freud on British Prime Minister Margaret Thatcher*

She sounded like the Book of Revelations read out over a railway station public address system by a headmistress of a certain age wearing calico knickers.
—*Clive James on Margaret Thatcher*

The Prime Minister tells us she has given the French president a piece of her mind, not a gift I would receive with alacrity.
—*Denis Healy on Margaret Thatcher*

If a traveler were informed that such a man was leader of the House of Commons, he may well begin to comprehend how the Egyptians worshipped an insect.
—*Benjamin Disraeli on Prime Minister Lord John Russell*

You read what Disraeli had to say. I don't remember what he said. He said something. He's no longer with us.
—*Bob Dole*

I have just read your dispatch about sore-tongued and fatigued horses. Will you pardon me for asking what the horses of your army have done since the battle of Antietam that fatigues anything?
—Abraham Lincoln in a telegram to
General George B. McClellan

My dear McClellan: If you don't want to use the army I should like to borrow it for a while. Yours respectfully, A. Lincoln.
—Abraham Lincoln to General George B. McClellan

My father always wanted to be the corpse at every funeral, the bride at every wedding, and the baby at every christening.
—Alice Roosevelt Longworth on Theodore Roosevelt

That is to say, he writes the worst English that I have ever
encountered. It reminds me of a string of wet sponges; it
reminds me of tattered washing on the line, it reminds me
of stale bean soup, of college yells, of dogs barking idiotically
through endless nights. It is so bad that a sort of grandeur creeps
into it. It drags itself out of the dark abysm of pish, and crawls
insanely up the topmost pinnacle of posh. It is rumble and bumble.
It is flap and doodle. It is balder and dash.

—*H. L. Mencken on Warren G. Harding*

According to the *L.A. Times*, Attorney General John Ashcroft wants
to take "a harder stance" on the death penalty. What's a harder stance
on the death penalty? We're already killing the guy! How do you
take a harder stance on the death penalty? What, are you going to
tickle him first? Give him itching powder? Put a thumbtack on the
electric chair?

—*Jay Leno*

How can they tell?

—Dorothy Parker, learning of Calvin Coolidge's death

He wouldn't commit himself to the time of day from a hatful
of watches.

—Westbrook Pegler on Herbert Hoover

This planet is our home. If we destroy the planet, we've destroyed
our home, so it is fundamentally important.

—H. Ross Perot

We'd like to avoid problems, because when we have problems, we can have troubles.

> —*Arizona Governor Wesley Bolin*

If he became convinced tomorrow that coming out for cannibalism would get him the votes he sorely needs, he would begin fattening a missionary in the White House backyard come Wednesday.

> —*H. L. Mencken on Franklin D. Roosevelt*

Ike didn't know anything, and all the time he was in office, he didn't learn a thing. . . . The general doesn't know any more about politics than a pig knows about Sunday.

> —*Harry Truman on Dwight D. Eisenhower*

He can compress the most words into the smallest ideas better than any man I ever met.

—*Abraham Lincoln, referring to a lawyer*

English was good enough for Jesus Christ and it's good enough for the children of Texas.

—*Miriam "Ma" Ferguson*

The main difference for the history of the world if I had been shot rather than Kennedy is that Onassis probably wouldn't have married Mrs. Khrushchev.

—*Nikita Khrushchev*

He turned out to be so many different characters he could have populated all of *War and Peace* and still had a few people left over.

—*Herbert Mitgang about Lyndon B. Johnson*

He inherited some good instincts from his Quaker forebears, but by diligent hard work, he overcame them.

—*James Reston on Richard Nixon*

Hell, if you work for Bill Clinton, you go up and down more times than a whore's nightgown.

—*White House advisor James Carville*

He can't help it—he was born with a silver foot in his mouth.
                    —*former Texas governor Ann Richards on George W. Bush*

Asking an incumbent member of Congress to vote for term limits is a bit like asking a chicken to vote for Colonel Sanders.
                                                            —*Bob Inglis*

Bush is smart. I don't think that Bush will ever be impeached, 'cause unlike Clinton, Reagan, or even his father, George W. is immune from scandal. Because, if George W. testifies that he had no idea what was going on, wouldn't you believe him?
                                                            —*Jay Leno*

V

LITERARY
LAMPOONS

You Can Make Up Almost Anything

Fiction writing is great. You can make up almost anything.
—*Ivana Trump, on finishing her first novel*

I'm all in favor of keeping dangerous weapons out of the hands of fools. Let's start with typewriters.
—*Frank Lloyd Wright*

It was a book to kill time for those who like it better dead.
—*Rose Macaulay*

A book is what they make a movie out of for television.

—*Leonard Levinson*

Paradise Lost is one of the books which the reader admires and puts down, and forgets to take up again. None ever wished it longer than it is.

—*Samuel Johnson, on Milton, from* Lives of the Poets

I wished to be near my mother.

—*James McNeil Whistler, when asked "Whatever possessed you to be born in a place like Lowell, Massachusetts?"*

There are only two tragedies in life: one is not getting what one wants, and the other is getting it.

—Oscar Wilde

A great many people now reading and writing would be better employed keeping rabbits.

—Edith Sitwell

The nice thing about egotists is that they don't talk about other people.

—source unknown

An editor should have a pimp for a brother so he'd have someone to look up to.

—*Gene Fowler*

I didn't like the play, but then I saw it under adverse conditions—the curtain was up.

—*Groucho Marx*

Nature, not content with denying him the ability to think, has endowed him with the ability to write.

—*A. E. Housman*

Thank you for sending me a copy of your book—I'll waste no time reading it.

—*Moses Hadas*

This is not a book that should be tossed lightly aside. It should be hurled with great force.

—*Dorothy Parker*

This is one of those big, fat paperbacks, intended to while away a monsoon or two, which, if thrown with a good overarm action, will bring a water buffalo to its knees.

>   —*Nancy Banks-Smith (review of M. M. Kaye's*
>   *The Far Pavilions)*

Alexander Woollcott had been asked to sign a first-edition copy of his book *Shouts and Murmurs*. "Ah, what is so rare as a Woollcott first edition?" he sighed as he wrote.

"A Woollcott second edition," replied Franklin P. Adams

A farm is an irregular patch of nettles bound by short-term notes, containing a fool and his wife who didn't know enough to stay in the city.

I began my career as a country squire with nothing but a high heart, a flask of citronella, and a fork for toasting marshmallows in case supplies ran low. In a scant fifteen years I have acquired a superb library of mortgages, mostly first editions, and the finest case of sacroiliac known to science. . . . I also learned that to lock horns with Nature, the only equipment you really need is the constitution of Paul Bunyan and the basic training of a commando. . . .

Today, thanks to unremitting study, I can change a fuse so deftly that it plunges the entire county into darkness. . . . The power company has offered me as high as fifteen thousand dollars a year to stay out of my own cellar.

—*S. J. Perelman*, Acres and Pains

There was only one catch, and that was Catch-22, which specified that a concern for one's safety in the face of dangers that were real and immediate was the process of a rational mind. Orr was crazy and could be grounded. All he had to do was ask; and as soon as he did, he would no longer be crazy and he would have to fly more missions. Orr would be crazy to fly more missions and sane if he didn't, but if he was sane he had to fly them. If he flew them he was crazy and didn't have to, but if he didn't want to, he was sane and had to.

—*Joseph Heller*, Catch-22

The starting point of this lecturing-trip around the world was Paris, where we had been living a year or two. We sailed for America, and there made certain preparations. This took but little time. Two members of my family elected to go with me. Also a carbuncle. The dictionary says a carbuncle is a kind of jewel. Humor is out of place in a dictionary.

—*Mark Twain*, Following the Equator

Men marry because they are tired; women, because they are curious; both are disappointed.

—*Oscar Wilde*

Marriage is popular because it combines the maximum of temptation with the maximum of opportunity.

—*George Bernard Shaw*

Marriage is like a cage; one sees the birds outside desperate to get in, and those inside desperate to get out.

—*Michel de Montaigne*

A husband is what is left of the lover after the nerve has
been extracted.

—*Helen Rowland*

This is no time for making new enemies.

—*Voltaire, when asked on his*
deathbed to renounce the Devil

By all means marry. If you get a good wife, you'll be happy. If you get
a bad one, you'll become a philosopher . . . and that is a good thing
for any man.

—*Socrates*

Don't give a woman advice; one should never give a woman anything she can't wear in the evening.

—*Oscar Wilde*

When a society has to resort to the lavatory for its humour, the handwriting is on the wall.

—*Alan Bennett*

All the world's a stage and most of us are desperately unrehearsed.

—*Sean O'Casey*

I have nothing against undertakers personally. It's just that I wouldn't want one to bury my sister.

— *Jessica Mitford*

I loathe people who keep dogs. They are cowards who haven't got the guts to bite people themselves.

—*August Strindberg*

Youth is a wonderful thing. What a crime to waste it on children.

—*George Bernard Shaw*

Big sisters are the crabgrass in the lawn of life.

—Charles Schulz

There are times when parenthood seems nothing but feeding the mouth that bites you.

—Peter DeVries

A bride at her second marriage does not wear a veil. She wants to see what she is getting.

—Helen Rowland

Many a man owes his success to his first wife and his second wife to his success.

—*Jim Backus*

I recently read that love is entirely a matter of chemistry. That must be why my wife treats me like toxic waste.

—*David Bissonette*

Cats are rather delicate creatures and they are subject to a good many ailments, but I never heard of one who suffered from insomnia.

—*Joseph Wood Krutch*

There are only two things a child will share willingly; communicable diseases and its mother's age.

—*Benjamin Spock*

I made my money the old fashioned way. I was very nice to a wealthy relative right before he died.

—*Malcom Forbes*

The best measure of a man's honesty isn't his income tax return. It's the zero adjust on his bathroom scale.

—*Arthur C. Clarke*

P. G. WODEHOUSE

The creator of the characters Jeeves and Wooster, Wodehouse (pronounced "Woodhouse") was one of the most admired twentieth century humorists.

There is only one cure for gray hair. It was invented by a Frenchman. It is called the guillotine.

She fitted into my biggest armchair as if it had been built round her by someone who knew they were wearing armchairs tight about the hips that season.

For an instance Wilfred Allsop's face lit up, as that of the poet Shelley whom he so closely resembled must have done when realised that "blithe spirit" rhymes with "near it," not that it does, and another ode as good as off the assembly line.

His first emotion was one of surprise that so much human tonnage could have been assembled at one spot. A cannibal king, beholding them, would have whooped with joy and reached for his knife and fork with the feeling that for once, the catering department had not failed him.

Poets, as a class, are business men. Shakespeare describes the poet's eye as rolling in a fine frenzy from heaven to earth, from earth to heaven, and giving to airy nothing a local habitation and a name, but in practice you will find that one corner of that eye is generally glued on the royalty returns.

AMBROSE BIERCE

Critic and commentator Bierce's The Devil's Dictionary *was originally called* The Cynic's Word Book. *Its entries deftly lampoon political and social conventions.*

adder. A species of snake. So called from its habit of adding funeral outlays to the other expenses of living

painting. The art of protecting flat surfaces from the weather and exposing them to the critic.

lawsuit. A machine which you go into as a pig and come out of as a sausage.

love. A temporary insanity curable by marriage.

egotist. (n.) A person of low taste, more interested in himself than in me.

pray. To ask the laws of the universe to be annulled on behalf of a single petitioner confessedly unworthy.

photograph. A picture painted by the sun without instruction in art.

sweater. (n.) Garment worn by child when its mother is feeling chilly.

VI

CLASSIC
JESTS

An All-Star Team of All-Time Favorites

A man tells his friend, "I've been making a lot of Freudian slips lately. For example, last week I asked the train conductor for two pickets to Tittsburgh."

"I did something similar the other day," says the friend. "My wife and I were having breakfast, and instead of saying, 'Honey, please pass the butter,' I said, 'You bitch, you ruined my life!'"

A Georgia state trooper pulled a car over some two miles south of the Georgia/South Carolina state line. The trooper asked the driver why he was speeding and learned he was a magician and a juggler on his way to Savannah to do a show that night at the Shrine Circus and didn't want to be late. The trooper told the driver he was fascinated by juggling, and if the driver would do a little juggling for him, he wouldn't get a ticket.

When the driver told the trooper he had sent all his equipment on ahead and didn't have anything to juggle, the trooper produced three flares from the patrol car's truck. The juggler lit them and proceeded to toss them into the air.

In the midst of the act, a car pulled in behind the patrol car. A good ol' boy who was plainly under the influence got out, observed the juggling, and staggered over to the patrol car, opened the rear door and got in.

The trooper walked over and asked the drunk where he thought he was going.

Explained the drunk, "You might as well haul my ass right to jail, because there's no way in hell I can pass that test."

A man bought a new rifle and took it out bear hunting. He spotted a small brown bear and shot it. Right after, there was a tap on his shoulder and he turned around to see a big black bear. The black bear said, "That was my cousin and you've got two choices: Either I maul you to death or we have sex."

The man realized he had no choice and agreed to the latter alternative. Even though he felt sore for two weeks, he vowed revenge.

On his next hunting trip he found the black bear and shot it. Immediately came a tap on his shoulder. A huge grizzly bear that was behind him said, "That was my cousin you killed. You've got two choices—either I maul you to death or we have rough sex." Again, the man realized he had no choice.

Although he survived, it took several months before the man finally recovered. As soon as he could, he returned to the woods, tracked down the grizzly and shot it.

Again, there was a tap on his shoulder. He turned to find a giant polar bear looking at him sadly and saying, "Admit it, mister—you don't come here for the hunting, do you?"

An Amish man and his young son left their farm to visit a shopping mall. They were amazed by everything they saw, but especially by two shiny, silver doors that slid apart and then slid back together again. The boy asked his father what it was, but his father, never having seen an elevator, had to admit that he had no idea.

The two watched as an elderly unattractive woman pressed the elevator button. The doors slid apart, she entered and the doors closed behind her. The two watched and waited several minutes until the doors opened and a beautiful young woman stepped out.

Without moving his eyes from the woman, the father said quietly to his son, "Hurry up and get your mother."

A teenaged girl tearfully breaks the news to her parents that she's missed two consecutive periods. Irate, the father screams, "I want whoever is responsible here—right now!"

The girl makes a phone call, and an hour later a Ferrari pulls up in front of the house. Out steps a distinguished middle-aged man in an Armani suit with a Rolex watch on his wrist. He is introduced to the parents, but before they can express their wrath, he says, "I admit I'm responsible for your daughter's condition. My family situation is such that I cannot marry her, but I'm more than willing to make provisions.

"If it's a boy, your daughter and he will be given a duplex on Park Avenue and a beach house in the Hamptons facing the water. The boy will receive five million dollars until he's eighteen, at which time he'll be given a factory to own and run.

"If it's a girl, your daughter and she will be given the duplex and the beach house. The girl will receive five million dollars until she's eighteen, at which time she'll be given a department store to own and run.

"If it's twins, each will be similarly provided for." Then the man paused, "But if your daughter has a miscarriage, I don't know what I'll do then."

At which point the father looks the man straight in the eye and says, "Then you'll sleep with her again."

An old cowboy sat down at the bar and ordered a drink. A few minutes later, a young woman sat down on the stool to his left. She turned and asked, "Are you a real cowboy?"

He replied, "Well, I've spent my whole life on ranches, breaking colts, working cows, going to rodeos, fixing fences, baling hay and doctoring calves, so, yes, I'd say I'm a cowboy. May I buy you a drink?"

"Thanks," the woman replied, "but I should tell you I'm a lesbian."

The cowboy looked puzzled. "What's a lesbian?"

"Well, I like women. I spend my whole day thinking about them. As soon as I get up in the morning, I think about women. When I shower, I think about women. When I watch TV, I think about women. I even think about women when I eat. It seems that every-thing makes me think of women."

A little while later, a man sat down on the bar stool to the cowboy's right. "Excuse me, but are you a real cowboy?"

"I always thought I was," the cowboy replied, "but I just found out I'm a lesbian."

Two men are walking down the street when a mugger demands their money. They both pull out their wallets and begin taking out their cash. Just then one man turns to the other and hands him a bill. "Here's that $20 I owe you," he says.

Stevie Wonder was invited to his first Passover seder. Handed a piece of matzoh, he rubbed his fingers across it and asked, "Who wrote this shit?"

A Texan visiting Israel told a native, "Compared to where I live, your country is nothing. Why, it takes me ten to fifteen hours to go across all the land I own."

"I totally understand," the Israeli says. "I used to have a car like that."

Two campers are walking through the woods when a huge brown bear suddenly appears in the clearing about 50 feet in front of them. The bear sees the campers and begins to head toward them. The first guy drops his backpack, digs out a pair of sneakers, and frantically begins to put them on. The second guy says, "What are you doing? Sneakers won't help you outrun that bear."

"I don't need to outrun the bear," the first guy says. "I just need to outrun you."

A lawyer dies and goes to Heaven. "There must be some mistake," the lawyer argues. "I'm too young to die. I'm only fifty-five."

"Fifty five?" says Saint Peter. "No, according to our calculations, you're eighty-two."

"How'd you get that?" the lawyer asks.

Answers St. Peter, "We added up your time sheets."

An old woman is upset at her husband's funeral. "You have him in a brown suit and I wanted him in a blue suit."

The mortician says, "We'll take care of it, ma'am," and yells back, "Ed, switch the heads on two and four!"

Two campers are hiking in the woods when one is bitten on the rear end by a rattlesnake. "I'll go into town for a doctor," the other says. He runs ten miles to a small town and finds the town's only doctor, who is delivering a baby.

"I can't leave," the doctor says. "But here's what to do. Take a knife, cut a little X where the bite is, suck out the poison and spit it on the ground." The guy runs back to his friend, who is in agony.

"What did the doctor say?" the victim asks.

"He says you're gonna die."

A duck goes into a bar, sits on the stool, and asks the bartender, "Do you have any grapes?"

The bartender patiently explains that he only serves drinks and maybe some pretzels or nuts, but no grapes.

The duck leaves.

The duck returns several days in a row, always asking the bartender the same question: "Do you have any grapes?"

The bartender becomes increasingly annoyed to the point that he finally says, "Hey duck, I told you I don't serve grapes. If you come in here one more time and ask for grapes, I'm gonna nail your bill to the bar."

The duck leaves.

Next day, the duck comes in, bellies up to the bar, and the bartender's ready for him. "What can I get you?" he says with a grimace.

The duck asks, "Do you have a hammer?"

The bartender shakes his head no.

The duck asks, "Do you have any grapes?"

A doctor had just bought a villa on the French Riviera, when he met an old lawyer friend whom he hadn't seen in years, and they started talking. The lawyer, as it turned out, owned a nearby villa. They discussed how they came to retire to the Riviera.

"Remember that lousy office complex I bought?" asked the lawyer. "Well, it caught fire, and I retired here with the fire insurance proceeds. What are you doing here?"

The doctor replied, "Remember that real estate I had in Germany? Well, the Rhine overflowed, and here I am with the flood insurance proceeds. It's amazing that we both ended up here pretty much the same way."

"It sure is," the lawyer replied, looking puzzled, "but I'm confused about one thing—how do you start a flood?"

A man goes skydiving for the first time. He jumps out of the airplane and, after waiting the prescribed time, pulls the ripcord. Nothing happens. He tries again. Still nothing. He starts to panic, but remembers his back-up chute. He pulls that cord. Nothing happens.

As he frantically pulls both cords, he looks down and sees another man flying up toward him. He yells, "Hey, do you know anything about skydiving?"

The other guy yells back, "No—do you know anything about gas stoves?"

A kindergarten teacher observing her classroom of children drawing walked up to a little girl who was working diligently. The teacher asked about her artwork. The girl replied, "I'm drawing God."

The teacher paused and said, "But no one knows what God looks like."

Without looking up from her drawing, the girl replied, "They will in a minute."

A three-year-old boy went with his father to see a litter of kittens. Returning home, the lad informed his mother that there were two boy kittens and two girl kittens. "How did you know?" his mother asked.

"Daddy picked them up, looked underneath, and told me," he replied. "I guess it's printed on the bottom."

Two men are out walking their dogs. It's a hot day, and they'd love to have a cold beer. They come across a bar, but in the window is a "no pets allowed" sign.

The man walking his German shepherd puts on a pair of sunglasses and enters the bar. The manager stops him, saying, "Sorry, no pets allowed."

The man replies, "You don't understand, this is my seeing-eye dog," and he is allowed inside.

The second man gets the idea. He too puts on a pair of sunglasses and walks in. He too is stopped by the manager, who tells him, "Sorry, but this bar doesn't allow pets."

The second man says, "You don't understand, this is my seeing-eye dog."

The manager says, "But that's a Chihuahua."

At which the man screams, "What? They gave me a goddamn *Chihuahua?*"

Two airline mechanics get off work at LaGuardia Airport in New York City. One says, "Let's go have a beer."

The other says, "Why don't we try drinking jet fuel? I hear it tastes like whiskey, and you don't have any hangover in the morning."

They each drink about a quart. The next morning, one mechanic phones the other and asks,

"Hey, how do you feel?"

"I feel great," the other replies.

"Me too. No hangover. Just one thing. Have you farted yet?"

"No," says his friend.

"Well then, don't—I'm calling from Phoenix!"

Two hunters are out in the woods when one of them collapses. He doesn't seem to be breathing and his eyes are glazed. The other man pulls out his phone and calls emergency services.

He gasps to the operator, "I think my friend is dead! What can I do?"

The operator in a calm, soothing voice replies, "Take it easy. I can help. First, let's make sure he's dead."

There is a silence, then a shot is heard. Back on the phone, the hunter says, "OK, now what?"

A woman gets on a bus with her baby. The bus driver says, "That's the ugliest baby that I've ever seen."

The woman goes to the rear of the bus and sits down, fuming. She says to a man next to her, "That driver just insulted me!"

The man says, "You go right up there and tell him off. Go ahead, I'll hold your monkey for you."

A minister assigned to a new church arrives on the day of a funeral for a man he never knew. He asks the bereaved family about the deceased, but no one had a good word to say. Stymied about what to do, the minister addressed the assembled mourners and asked whether anyone in the church had a few words in praise of the deceased.

After a long pause, from the back of the church a voice called out, "His brother was even worse!"

MURPHY'S LAWS

Murphy's Law, which posits that "If anything can go wrong, it will," is named for Captain Edward A. Murphy, an engineer working on a project at Edwards Air Force Base in 1949. Finding something that had gone amiss, he said of the person who had caused the error, "If there is any way to do it wrong, he'll find it." By extension, the phrase "Murphy's Law" is now used to speculate about error-prone situations.

Murphy's Education Laws

- The classroom clock is always wrong.

- The time a teacher takes in explaining is inversely proportional to the information retained by students.

- The problem child will be a school board member's son.

- When reviewing your notes before an exam, the most important ones will be illegible.

- If you are given an open-book exam, you will forget your book.

Murphy's Computer Laws

- Any given program, when running, is obsolete.

- Any given program costs more and takes longer.

- If a program is useful, it will have to be changed.

- If a program is useless, it will have to be documented.

- Any program will expand to fill available memory.

Murphy's Child-Raising Laws:

- When you need to carry a child, he or she will want to walk.

- When you want them to walk, they will want to be carried.

- When you bring the stroller, they will want to walk.

- When you forget the stroller, they will want to ride.

- A child will fall asleep in the car five minutes before you reach your destination.

Murphy's Automobile Laws

- Washing your car constitutes a rain dance to the raining gods.

- The temperature of seat covers is inversely proportional to the length of your skirt or shorts.

- Your car keys are always in the pocket on the side of your hand that is carrying more things.

- The shortest route between two points will be under construction.

- The louder the car alarm, the more likely everyone but the owner will hear it.

M
U
R
P
H
Y
,
S

L
A
W
S

VII

MUSIC DROLLERIES

Better Than It Sounds

Wagner's music is better than it sounds.

—Mark Twain

He'd be better off shoveling snow.

—Richard Strauss on Arnold Schoenberg

[Richard] Wagner has beautiful moments but bad quarters of an hour.

—Gioacchino Rossini

Dr. Johnson was observed by a musical friend of his to be extremely inattentive at a concert, whilst a celebrated solo player was running up the divisions and subdivisions of notes upon his violin. His friend, to induce him to take greater notice of what was going on, told him how extremely difficult it was. "Difficult do you call it, sir?"

Replied the doctor, "I wish it were impossible."
> —*John Boswell*, Life of Samuel Johnson

Jacques Thibault, the violinist, was once handed an autograph book by a fan while in the green room after a concert. "There's not much room on this page," he said. "What shall I write?"

Another violinist overheard the question. "Write your repertoire," he suggested. "I can wait."
> —*Arnold Schoenberg, who was once told that a soloist would need six fingers to perform his concerto*

His music used to be original. Now it's aboriginal.

—*Sir Ernest Newman on Igor Stravinsky*

If he'd been making shell-cases during the war it might have been better for music.

—*Maurice Ravel on Camille Saint-Saens*

He has an enormously wide repertory. He can conduct anything, provided it's by Beethoven, Brahms or Wagner. He tried Debussy's *La Mer* once. It came out as *Das Merde*.

—*anonymous musician on conductor George Szell*

Never look at the trombones; it only encourages them.

—*Richard Strauss*

Someone commented to Rudolph Bing, manager of the Metropolitan Opera, that George Szell is his own worst enemy. "Not while I'm alive, he isn't!" said Bing.

We cannot expect you to be with us all the time, but perhaps you could be good enough to keep in touch now and again.

—*Sir Thomas Beecham to a musician during a rehearsal*

Already too loud!
—*Bruno Walter at his first rehearsal with an American orchestra,
on seeing the players reaching for their instruments*

MTV is to music as KFC is to chicken.

—*Lewis Black*

If your lifeguard duties were as good as your singing, a lot of people
would be drowning.

—*Simon Cowell, American Idol judge*

BAD-MOUTHING INSTRUMENTS AND THE MUSICIANS WHO PLAY THEM

Q: How do you protect a valuable instrument?

A: Hide it in an accordion case.

Q: What is the definition of an optimist?

A: An accordion player with a pager.

Q. How do you get two bagpipes to play a perfect unison?

A. Shoot one.

Q: Why do bagpipers march when they play?

A: To get away from the noise.

Q: Why is the banjo player a fiddle player's best friend?

A: Without him, the fiddle would be the most hated instrument on earth.

Q: How can you tell the difference among all those banjo tunes?

A: Only by their names.

Q: Why did the bass player get mad at the timpanist?

A: He turned one of the bass's tuning pegs and wouldn't tell the bass player which one.

Q: How many bass players does it take to change a light bulb?

A: None. The piano player can do that with his left hand.

Q: What is the difference between the first and last desk of a viola section?

A. Half a measure.

Q: Why are orchestra intermissions limited to twenty minutes?

A: So you don't have to retrain the cellists.

Q: How do you get a cellist to play fortissimo?

A: Write *pp, espressivo.*

Q: How do you know if there is a percussionist at the door?

A: The knocking gets slower.

Q: How can you tell when there is a drummer at your front door?

A: The knocking gets faster.

Q: How do you know when a drum solo's really bad?

A: The bass player notices.

Q: How do you make a trombone sound like a French horn?

A: Put your hand in the bell and miss a lot of notes.

Q: How do you make a violin sound like a viola?

A: Sit in the back and don't play.

Q: How do you make a violin sound like a viola?

A: Play in the low register with a lot of wrong notes.

Q: How do horn players traditionally greet each other?

A: "Hi. I did that piece in junior high."

Q: What do you call two guitarists playing in unison?

A: Counterpoint.

Q: How do you get a guitar player to play softer?

A: Give him a sheet of music.

Q: What's the difference between trumpet players and government bonds?

A: Government bonds eventually mature and earn money.

Q. What is the best recording of the Haydn Trumpet Concerto?

A. Music Minus One.

Q: What is the difference between a Wagnerian soprano and an NFL offensive lineman?

A: Stage makeup.

GRADE-SCHOOL MUSIC TESTS

The principal singer of nineteenth-century opera was called pre-Madonna.

It is easy to teach anyone to play the maracas. Just grip the neck and shake him in rhythm.

Gregorian chant has no music, just singers singing the same lines.

Sherbet composed the Unfinished Symphony.

All female parts were sung by castrati. We don't know exactly what they sounded like because there are no known descendants.

Young scholars have expressed their rapture for the *Bronze Lullaby,* the *Taco Bell Cannon,* Beethoven's *Erotica,* Tchaikovsky's *Cracknutter Suite,* and Gershwin's *Rap City in Blue.*

Music sung by two people at the same time is called a duel; if they sing without music it is called Acapulco.

A virtuoso is a musician with real high morals.

Diatonic is a low calorie Schweppes.

Probably the most marvelous fugue was the one between the Hatfields and the McCoys.

A harp is a nude piano.

The main trouble with a French horn is that it is too tangled up.

An interval in music is the distance from one piano to the next.

The correct way to find the key to a piece of music is to use
a pitchfork.

Agitato is a state of mind when one's finger slips in the middle of
playing a piece.

Refrain means don't do it. A refrain in music is the part you'd better
not try to sing.

I know what a sextet is but I'd rather not say.

Most authorities agree that music of antiquity was written long ago.

My favorite composer was Opus. Agnus Dei was a woman composer famous for her church music.

Henry Purcell was a well-known composer few people have ever heard of.

VIII

QUIPS
HEARD
AROUND
THE WORLD

A Palm Tree in Dakota

Transplanting the ballet to the United States is like trying to raise a palm tree in Dakota.

—*Lincoln Kirsten*

I found [America] a country with thirty-two religions and only one sauce.

—*Charles-Maurice de Talleyrand-Perigord*

Half of the American people have never read a newspaper. Half never voted for President. One hopes it is the same half.

—*Gore Vidal*

Germans are flummoxed by humor, the Swiss have no concept of fun, the Spanish think there is nothing at all ridiculous about eating dinner at midnight, and the Italians should never, ever have been let in on the invention of the motor car.

—*Bill Bryson*

It is quite untrue that British people don't appreciate music. They may not understand it but they absolutely love the noise it makes.

—*Sir Thomas Beecham*

In America, only the successful writer is important, in France all writers are important, in England no writer is important, and in Australia you have to explain what a writer is.

—*Geoffrey Cottrell*

There have been many definitions of hell, but for the English the best definition is that it is the place where the Germans are the police, the Swedish are the comedians, the Italians are the defense force, Frenchmen dig the roads, the Belgians are the pop singers, the Spanish run the railways, the Turks cook the food, the Irish are the waiters, the Greeks run the government, and the common language is Dutch.

—*David Frost and Anthony Jay*

France is a country where the money falls apart but you can't tear the toilet paper.

—*Billy Wilder*

German is the most extravagantly ugly language—it sounds like someone using a sick bag on a 747.

—*Willy Rushton*

The food in Yugoslavia is fine if you like pork tartare.

—*Ed Begley, Jr.*

I love Thanksgiving turkey . . . it's the only time in Los Angeles that you see natural breasts.

—*Arnold Schwarzenegger*

I know why the sun never sets on the British Empire: God wouldn't trust an Englishman in the dark.

—Duncan Spaeth

When it's three o'clock in New York, it's still 1938 in London.

—Bette Midler

The Irish are a fair people, they never speak well of one another.

—Samuel Johnson

Like an Irishman's obligation, all on the one side, and always yours.

—English saying

The trouble with Ireland is that it's a country full of genius, with absolutely no talent.

—Hugh Leonard

The great thing about Glasgow now is that if there is a nuclear attack it'll look exactly the same afterwards.

—Billy Connolly

He who would eat in Spain must bring his kitchen along.

—*German saying*

One thing I will say about the Germans, they are always perfectly willing to give somebody's land to somebody else.

—*Will Rogers*

Because of their cuisine, Germans don't consider farting rude. They'd certainly be out of luck if they did.

—*P. J. O'Rourke*

I found the pearl of the Orient slightly less exciting than a rainy Sunday evening in Rochester.

—*S. J. Perelman*

It is after you have lost your teeth that you can afford to buy steaks.

—*Pierre Renoir*

I fear that I have not got much to say about Canada, not having seen much; what I got by going to Canada was a cold.

—*Henry David Thoreau*

The reason there are so many tree-lined boulevards in Paris is so the German Army can march in the shade.

—attributed to General George Patton

Other people have a nationality. The Irish and the Jews have a psychosis.

—Brendan Behan

No one can be as calculatedly rude as the British, which amazes Americans, who do not understand studied insult and can only offer abuse as a substitute.

—Paul Gallico

The English country gentleman galloping after a fox—the unspeakable in full pursuit of the uneatable.

—*Oscar Wilde*

The French are sawed-off sissies who eat snails and slugs and cheese that smells like people's feet. Utter cowards who force their own children to drink wine, they gibber like baboons even when you try to speak to them in their own wimpy language.

—*P. J. O'Rourke*

In Russia a man is called reactionary if he objects to having his property stolen and his wife and children murdered.

—*Winston Churchill*

FUNNY CURSES

Yiddish

He should grow upside down with his head in the ground like a turnip.

All problems I have in my heart should go to his head.

He should give it all away to doctors.

He should have a large store, and whatever people ask for he shouldn't have, and what he does have shouldn't be requested.

Irish

May the curse of Mary Malone and her nine blind illegitimate children chase you so far over the hills of Damnation that the Lord himself can't find you with a telescope.

Chinese

I wish you a slow death, but a quick ride to hell!

IX

ETHNIC JOKES

"Iceberg, Goldberg—What's the Difference?"

A Chinese man and his Jewish friend were walking along one day when the Jewish man whirled and slugged the Chinese man. "What was that for?" the Chinese man asked.

"For what you people did to Pearl Harbor."

"Pearl Harbor? That was the Japanese. I'm Chinese."

"Chinese, Japanese—what's the difference?"

They continued walking and after a while the Chinese man whirled and knocked the Jewish man to the ground. "What was that for?" the Jewish man asked.

"For what you did to the *Titanic*."

"The *Titanic*? That was an iceberg."

"Iceberg, Goldberg—what's the difference?"

A German, an American, and a Mexican are traveling in Brazil and are captured by hostile natives. The head of the tribe asks the German, "What do you want on your back for your whipping?"

The German responds, "I will take oil!" So they put oil on his back, and a villager whips him ten times. When he is finished, the German has huge welts on his back and can hardly move.

The Mexican is asked what he wants on his back. "I will take nothing!" says the Mexican, and he takes his ten lashes without flinching.

"And what will you have on your back?" the American is asked.

He responds, "The Mexican."

In revolutionary Paris, 1789, three Irish spies are about to be guillotined. "Do you want to be beheaded on your back or your front?" the executioner asked O'Brien.

"On my front," said O'Brien. He was placed on his front, the executioner pulled the lever, but the blade jammed. O'Brien was reprieved because no man can be sentenced to death twice.

Hoskins, who was next, also chose to die facedown. Again the blade jammed, and Hoskins was reprieved.

Murphy was third. "Back or front?" he was asked.

"I'm not afraid—place me on my back."

Murphy was laid on his back under the blade. "Begorrah," he said, looking up. "Wait a minute—I think I can see why it jams."

Pat and Mike were doing some street repairs in front of a known house of ill repute in Boston. A rabbi came walking down the street, looked furtively in both directions and then ducked into the house.

Pat paused a bit from swinging his pick and said, "Mike, will you look at that! A man of the cloth, and going into a place like that in broad daylight!"

A while later, a minister came down the street, looked to the left and right, and scurried into the house. Mike laid his shovel down, turned to Pat and said, "Pat! Are you seeing what I'm seeing? A man of the church, and he's giving that place his custom."

Just then a priest came down the street and slipped into the bawdy house.

Pat and Mike straightened up, removed their hats, and Mike said, "Faith, and there must be somebody close to death in there."

Then there was the Irishman who sued the local baker for forging the Irishman's signature on a hot cross bun.

A panhandler approached a Jewish mother on the street and said, "Lady, I haven't eaten in three days."

"Force yourself," she replied.

The headmistress of a Mississippi seminary for young ladies decided to hold a dinner-dance. Seeking escorts, she called the colonel of the local army base and requested twenty-four fine young gentlemen, then added confidentially, "Now, I understand you have many soldiers from New York. My young ladies come from the finest families in the South, so I would be obliged if you wouldn't send any Jewish soldiers."

"Not to worry, ma'am," replied the colonel.

The evening of the dinner-dance, a bus from the base pulled up to the seminary's front door and out came two dozen African American soldiers.

When the headmistress recovered her voice, she gasped, "There . . . there must be some mistake."

"No, ma'am," said one of the soldiers, "Colonel Goldberg never makes mistakes."

A Jewish man lives in California and is feeling guilty about not visiting his mother in New York for a long time, so on her birthday he decides to get her a special gift. He goes to a pet store and buys a parrot that can speak four different languages. He has the bird shipped to his mother so that it arrives on the morning of her birthday.

That evening he calls his mother to wish her a happy birthday. "So, Ma, did you get the parrot?"

"Yes. Thank you, Jerry," his mother says.

"So, Ma, what did you think of the bird?" he asks.

His mother replies, "I had it for dinner. It was delicious."

The son is amazed. "Ma, you ate the bird? That was a rare parrot. It spoke four languages."

The mother shrugged. "He should have said something."

There is a big controversy on when life actually begins. In Jewish tradition, the fetus is not considered viable until it graduates from medical school.

The innkeeper loves the drunkard, but not for a son-in-law.
—*Yiddish Proverb*

A Mafioso finds out that his bookkeeper has screwed him for ten million dollars. This bookkeeper is deaf, an occupational benefit since it was assumed that a deaf bookkeeper would not be able to hear anything he'd ever have to testify about in court.

When the Mafioso confronts the bookkeeper about his missing money, he brings along his attorney, who knows sign language. The Mafioso asks, "Where's the ten million bucks you embezzled from me?" The attorney, using sign language, asks the bookkeeper, and the bookkeeper signs back. The attorney tells the Mafioso, "He says he doesn't know what you're talking about."

The Mafioso pulls out a 9-mm pistol, puts it to the bookkeeper's temple, cocks it, and says, "Ask him again!"

The attorney signs, "Don Vito will kill you for sure if you don't tell him!"

The bookkeeper sighs and signs back, "Okay, you win. The money is in a brown briefcase buried behind the shed in my cousin Enzo's backyard on Staten Island."

The Mafioso asks the attorney, "Well, what'd he say?"

The attorney shakes his head. "He says you don't have the guts to pull the trigger."

As an elderly Italian man lay on his deathbed, he suddenly smelled the aroma of his favorite Italian anisette-sprinkled cookies wafting up the stairs. He gathered his remaining strength, and lifted himself from the bed. Leaning against the wall, he slowly made his way out of the bedroom, and with even greater effort, gripping the railing with both hands, he crawled downstairs. With labored breath, he leaned against the door frame, gazing into the kitchen.

There spread out on waxed paper on the kitchen table were literally hundreds of his favorite anisette-sprinkled cookies. Mustering one great final effort, he staggered toward the table and reached out a hand.

Suddenly a spatula smacked his hand. "Back off!" his wife told him. "They're for the funeral."

A young Italian man excitedly tells his mother he's fallen in love and that he is going to get married. "Just for fun, Mama, I'm going to bring over three women and you try and guess which one I'm going to marry." His mother agrees.

The next day, he brings three beautiful women who chat for an hour with his mother. The son returns and says, "Okay Mama, which one am I going to marry?"

The mother replies with no hesitation, "The one on the right."

"That's amazing, Ma—you're right!" says the son. "How did you know?"

The mother replies, "Her I don't like."

At an auction in Edinburgh a wealthy American announced that he had lost his wallet containing £10,000 and would give a reward of £100 to the person who found it.

From the back of the hall a Scottish voice shouted, "I'll give £150!"

A man walks into a pub with an octopus. He sits the octopus down on a stool and tells everyone that the octopus can play any musical instrument in the world. Everyone laughs, so the man says he'll bet $50.00 to anyone who has an instrument that the octopus can't play.

Someone hands the octopus a guitar, which the octopus plays better than Eric Clapton. Someone then hands the octopus a trumpet that the octopus plays better than Miles Davis.

A Scotsman walks up with a set of bagpipes. The octopus fumbles with them for a minute and then sits down with a confused look.

"Ha, ha!" the Scot says. "Ye canna plae it, can ye?"

The octopus looks up at him and says, "Play it? Once I figure out how to get its pajamas off, I'm going to screw its brains out."

As a senior citizen was driving down a British motorway, his car phone rang. Answering, he heard his wife's voice urgently warning him, "Nigel, I just heard on the news that there's a car going the wrong way on the A-30. Please be careful!"

"Hell," said her husband, "not just one car—it's hundreds of them!"

Two men are sitting on the front porch at an English nudist colony. One turns to the other and asks, "I say, old boy, have you read Marx?"

The other replies, "Yes, I believe it's these wicker chairs."

Three proofs—
Equal-opportunity slurs

THREE PROOFS THAT JESUS WAS JEWISH

He went into his father's business.

He lived at home until he was thirty.

He was sure his mother was a virgin, and his mother thought he was God.

THREE PROOFS THAT JESUS WAS IRISH

He never got married.

He was always telling stories.

He loved green pastures.

THREE PROOFS THAT JESUS WAS PUERTO RICAN

His first name was Jesus.

He was bilingual.

He was always being harassed by the authorities.

THREE PROOFS THAT JESUS WAS ITALIAN

He talked with his hands.

He had wine with every meal.

He worked in the building trades.

THREE PROOFS THAT JESUS WAS BLACK

He called everybody "brother."

He liked Gospel.

He couldn't get a fair trial.

THREE PROOFS THAT JESUS WAS A CALIFORNIAN

He never cut his hair.

He walked around barefoot.

He started a new religion.

THREE PROOFS THAT JESUS WAS A WOMAN

He had to feed a crowd, at a moment's notice, when there was no food.

He kept trying to get the message across to a bunch of men who just didn't get it.

Even when he was dead, he had to get up because there was more work to do.

X

WORDPLAY

Beyond My Apprehension

Malapropisms

Mrs. Malaprop (her name means "inappropriate") was a character in Richard Sheridan's 1775 play, The Rivals. *She has lent her name to the variety of verbal miscues, such as:*

Promise to forget this fellow—to illiterate [obliterate] him, I say, quite from your memory.

He is the very pineapple [pinnacle] of politeness!

I have since laid Sir Anthony's preposition [proposition] before her.

Oh! It gives me the hydrostatics [hysterics] to such a degree.

He's as headstrong as an allegory [alligator] on the banks of the Nile.

I thought she had persisted [desisted] from corresponding with him.

His physiognomy [phraseology] is so grammatical!

and from her heirs and successors:

If we have offended any Christians I would ask them to forgive us,
which seems to be one of the main tenements in the New Testament.
                    —*Paul Bettany, on* The DaVinci Code *film*

It is beyond my apprehension.

—Danny Ozark, baseball team manager

I cannot tell you how grateful I am—I am filled with humidity.

—Gib Lewis, speaker of the Texas House of Representatives

This is unparalyzed in the state's history.

—Gib Lewis, Texas Speaker of the House

And then he [Mike Tyson] will have only channel vision.

—*Frank Bruno, boxer*

Marie Scott . . . has really plummeted to the top.

—*Alan Weeks*

He's going up and down like a metronome.

—*Ron Pickering*

Without further adieu.

—*source unknown*

He was a man of great statue.

—*Thomas Menino, Boston mayor*

Well, that was a cliff-dweller.

—*Wes Westrum, about a close baseball game*

If Gower had stopped that [cricket ball] he would have decapitated his hand.

—*Farokh Engineer*

We seem to have unleased a hornet's nest.

—*Valerie Singleton*

This series has been swings and pendulums all the way through.

—*Trevor Bailey, cricket commentator*

It's got lots of installation.

—Mike Smith, describing his new coat

It's a proven fact that capital punishment is a detergent to crime.

—Archie Bunker, All in the Family

Men think monogamy is something you make dining tables out of.

—Kathy Lette

SPOONERISMS

A transposition of initial letters, spoonerisms derive their name from the Reverend William Archibald Spooner (1844–1930), a British clergyman who became legendary for such slips of the tongue. Among his best known examples are "The lord is a shoving leopard" (instead of "loving shepherd"), "It is kisstomary to cuss the bride," and "Mardon me padam, this pie is occupewed. Can I sew you to another sheet?"

As a warden at Oxford University, he reprimanded a student for "fighting a liar in the quadrangle." To another student who "hissed my mystery lecture," Dr. Spooner said in disgust, "You have tasted two worms."

At a dinner at Oxford, Dr. Spooner proposed a toast that should have begun with "Let us raise our glasses and toast the dear Queen", but came out with instead, "Let us glaze our asses and toast the queer Dean."

At a naval review Dr. Spooner marveled at "this vast display of cattle ships and bruisers." Visiting a friend's country cottage, he complimented his host with, "You have a nosy little cook here."

Two years before his death, Dr. Spooner said he could recall only one such error, when the hymn "Conquering Kings Their Titles Take" came out "Kinkering Kongs."

Among celebrated Spoonerisms . . .

Newscaster Lowell Thomas presented British minister Sir Stafford Cripps as Sir Stifford Crapps.

During a radio broadcast of the Metropolitan Opera led by Arturo Toscanini, the announcer said, "This afternoon we are fortunate in having the distinguished conductor Antino Toscanuri . . . ah, Anturo Toscaniri." [The announcer paused, and then continued with "Ladies and gentlemen, my name is Milton J. Cross. Please remember it because you won't ever hear it again."]

At the inauguration of President Herbert Hoover, the radio newscaster proclaimed, "The next voice you hear will be that of our new president, Hoobert Heever." [The broadcaster was Harry Von Zell, later and better known as the announcer of *The Burns and Allen Show*.]

A radio reporter spoke about the World War Two "battle of the Bulgian Belch" (Belgian bulge).

A BBC announcer introduced someone as "a Transpert Export, sorry, Transport Expert."

A Dallas radio announcer advertising Lightcrust bread said, "Lightcrust, makers of the breast in bed . . ."

and a few others:

uphold the American lay of wife (way of life)

Battery Porn (Pottery Barn)

go in with buns glazing! (guns blazing)

Shall We Rather at the Giver? (the hymn "Shall We Gather at the River?")

Birthington's washday (Washington's Birthday)

one swell foop (one fell swoop)

chewing the doors (doing the chores)

mean as custard (keen as mustard)

rental deceptionist (dental receptionist)

and the eminently obvious . . . *A Sale of Two Titties* by Darles Chickens

NEWSPAPER HEADLINES . . . AMBIGUOUS, ERRONEOUS, AND JUST PLAIN DOPEY

Something Went Wrong in Jet Crash, Expert Says

Police Begin Campaign to Run Down Jaywalkers

Safety Experts Say School Bus Passengers Should be Belted

Drunk Gets Nine Months in Violin Case

Survivor of Siamese Twins Joins Parents

Iraqi Head Seeks Arms

British Left Waffles on Falkland Islands

Eye Drops off Shelf

Teacher Strikes Idle Kids

Reagan Wins on Budget, but More Lies Ahead

Shot Off Woman's Leg Helps Nicklaus to 66

Plane Too Close to Ground, Crash Probe Told

Miners Refuse to Work After Death

Stolen Painting Found by Tree

Couple Slain: Police Suspect Homicide

Red Tape Holds Up New Bridge

Astronaut Takes Blame for Gas in Spacecraft

Hospitals are Sued by 7 Foot Doctors

Some Pieces of Rock Hudson Sold at Auction

Include Your Children When Baking Cookies

Mondegreens

Mondegreens are misheard song lyrics, the word coming from someone's having misheard a line from an old Scots ballad "The Bonny Earl of Moray": "Ye Highland and ye Lowlands,/ Oh, where have ye been?/They have slain the Earl of Moray/And laid him on the green" was taken to be " . . . They have slain the Earl of Moray/And Lady Mondegreen."

"Jose, can you see . . ." instead of "Oh, say can you see . . ." ["The Star Spangled Banner"]

"O Canada, our home's on naked land" instead of "our home and native land" ["O Canada"]

"The girl with colitis goes by" instead of "The girl with kaleidoscope eyes" ["Lucy in the Sky with Diamonds" by The Beatles]

"'Scuse me while I kiss this guy," instead of "'Scuse me while I kiss the sky" ["Purple Haze" by Jimi Hendrix]

"I'll never leave the pizza burnin'" instead of "I'll never be your beast of burden" ["Beast of Burden" by The Rolling Stones]

"Give me the Beach Boys and free my soul" instead of "Give me the beat, boys, and free my soul" ["Drift Away" by Dobie Gray]

"Donuts make my brown eyes blue" instead of the title line of ["Don't It Make My Brown Eyes Blue"]

". . . blessed art thou, a monk swimming" [from the Hail Mary phrase "blessed art thou amongst women"]

"Gladly, the cross-eyed bear" instead of "Gladly the cross 'd bear"
["Keep Thou My Way"]

"Lead on O kinky turtle" instead of the first line of the hymn
["Lead on O King Eternal"]

"Olive, the other reindeer" instead of "all of the other reindeer"
["Rudolph the Red-Nosed Reindeer"]

"Barney's the king of Israel" instead of "Born is the king of Israel"
["The First Noel"]

"Round John Virgin" instead of "Round yon virgin mother and child"
["Silent Night"]

"I'm not talkin' 'bout Chlamydia" instead of "I'm not talkin' 'bout movin' in" ["I'd Really Love To See You Tonight"]

"Why can't I feed you dopamine" instead of "Why can't I free your doubtful mind" ["Cold, Cold Heart"]

Although not properly a Mondegreen because it's not a song lyric, an early computer speech-recognition program came out with "It Is hard to wreck a nice beach" for "It's hard to recognize speech."

Puns

The pun is the lowest form of humor . . . that is, if you didn't think of it first.

A botanist seeking information on a particular kind of fern sent a request to colleagues. He failed to be sufficiently specific, so his fax machine was quickly disgorging correspondence about every type of fern but the one about which he wanted to know. That's why he sent a follow-up message: If it ain't bracken, don't fax it.

Two Eskimos sitting in a kayak were chilly, but when they lit a fire in the craft, it sank—proving once and for all that you can't have your kayak and heat it, too.

Two boll weevils grew up in Mississippi. One went to Hollywood and became a famous actor. The other stayed behind in the cotton fields and never amounted to much, and was known locally as the lesser of the two weevils.

A Viking explorer returned home to find his name missing from the town register. The appropriate official apologized profusely, explaining, "I don't know how that happened—I must have taken Leif off my census."

Shortly after the Korean War, the son of South Korean President Syngman Rhee was hired as a *Life* magazine correspondent. The younger Rhee was a remarkably kind, gentle and considerate man, but he had a drinking problem. On one occasion, he was on a three-day bender when a colleague who had been sent on a search mission finally spotted him in a bar and said, "Ah, sweet Mr. Rhee of *Life*, at last I've found you."

Simon and Garth took their dog Walter to their uncle's mansion. It was raining when they left so they were offered the use of their relative's car and driver. The driver's large size bothered the dog, which began to bark. The butler explained the disturbance to the maid, with "Simon and Garth's uncle's big chauffeur's troubled Walter."

Two atoms are walking down the street and they run into each other. One says to the other, "Are you all right?"

"No, I lost an electron!"

"Are you sure?" the first asked.

"Yeah," said the other, "I'm positive!"

A chain of Elvis Presley steak houses appeals to diners who love meat tender.

A forger of postage stamps received the harshest sentence of any felon last year, proving that imitation is the sinisterest form of philately.

Then there was the Buddhist who refused novocaine during root canal work because he wanted to transcend dental medication.

A dentist chastised a patient for having eaten too much Hollandaise sauce, the acidity of which corroded his dentures. Explained the dentist, "I'll have to install a new plate made of chrome this time."

"Why chrome?"" the man asked.

"Because there's no plate like chrome for the Hollandaise."

Some securities analysts have correlated stock market prices to rise and fall with the hemlines of ladies' skirts and dresses. For example, hot pants led the Dow Jones up in 1971; stocks and miniskirts soared in 1993; stocks and hemlines went down in the spring of 1994.

The conclusion: "Don't be a buyer till you see the heights of their thighs!"

A group of chess enthusiasts checked into a hotel and were standing in the lobby discussing their recent tournament victories. Someone who overhead them complained about the chess nuts boasting in an open foyer.

A hungry lion roaming through the jungle came across two men. One sat under a tree reading a book; the other was typing away on a laptop. The lion quickly devoured only the man reading the book because he knew that readers digest, but writers cramp.

A patient told his psychiatrist, "Doctor, I keep having these alternating recurring dreams. First I'm a teepee; then I'm a wigwam; then I'm a teepee; then I'm a wigwam. It's driving me crazy. What's wrong with me?" The doctor replied, "First of all, relax—you're two tents."

A biologist studying amphibians discovered that the world's frog population was declining at an alarming rate. A chemist colleague discovered the remedy. Because of a chemical change in swamp water, frogs couldn't stay coupled long enough to reproduce successfully. The chemist then created an adhesive to assist the frogs' togetherness that included one part sodium. It worked, because the frogs needed monosodium glue to mate.

Then there was the angel who forgot to take her instrument with her after spending an evening at a nightclub owned by a bivalve. She left her harp in Sam Clam's disco.

After retiring as a nanny, Mary Poppins moved to Hollywood, where she opened a fortune-teller parlor, where she developed a premonition whenever someone was about to have an onset of bad breath. To publicize this skill, Ms. Poppins placed a sign in the window: SUPER CALIFORNIA MYSTIC EXPERT HALITOSIS.

A fisherman out in a boat on a crystal-clear lake dropped his wallet into the water. As it sank, he saw a carp came along and snatched it. Another carp appeared and grabbed the wallet while another fish waited for its chance. The fisherman exclaimed aloud, "Hmm, carp-to-carp walleting."

A woman gave up twin baby boys for adoption. One of them went to an Arab family that named the child Amal. The other went to a Hispanic family that named their son Juan. Years later, Juan sends a picture of himself to his birth mother, who looks at the picture and then tells her husband that she wishes she had a photo of the other child too. Her husband replies, "Why bother? When you've seen Juan, you've seen Amal."

Two peanuts walked through a tough section of town, and one was assaulted.

There were three Native American squaws. One slept on a deer skin, another on an elk skin, and the third slept on a hippopotamus skin. All three became pregnant. Two had baby boys, while the one who slept on the hippopotamus skin had twins. Which proves the theorum that the squaw of the hippopotamus is equal to the sons of the squaws of the other two hides.

A frog goes into a bank and approaches the teller. He can see from her name plate that the teller's name is Patricia Whack. The frog says, "Ms. Whack, I'd like to get a loan to buy a boat and go on a long vacation."

She looks at the frog in disbelief and asks how much he wants to borrow. The frog says $30,000. The teller asks his name and the frog says it's Kermit Jagger and that it's okay—he knows the bank manager.

She explains that $30,000 is a substantial amount of money and that he will need to secure some collateral against the loan. She asks if he has anything to use as collateral.

"Sure," the frog says and produces a tiny pink porcelain elephant about half an inch tall.

Very confused, the teller explains that she'll have to consult the bank manager and disappears into a back office. She finds the manager and says, "There's a frog out there called Kermit Jagger who claims to know you and wants to borrow $30,000. And he wants to use this as collateral." She holds up the tiny pink elephant. "I mean, what the heck is this?"

The bank manager looks her in the eye and says, "It's a knickknack, Patti Whack. Give the frog a loan. His old man's a Rolling Stone."

XI

KID
STUFF

Knock, Knock, Yo' Mama

Q & As

Q. How do you catch a school of fish?

A. With a bookworm!

Q. Why does a bee have sticky hair?

A. Because it uses a honeycomb!

Q. What do you call a sheep covered with chocolate?

A. A Hershey Baaaaaaaaa!

Q. Which Peter Pan character never took a bath?

A. Stinkerbell.

Q. Why don't candle trimmers work every day?

A. They only work on wick-ends.

Q. What do ghost owls cry?

A. Boo-Whoo!

Q: Why did the pony cough?

A: He was a little hoarse.

Q. What do you call a car with worn-out wheels?

A. Tired.

Q: What do sheep do on sunny days?

A: Have a baa-baa-cue.

Q. Why did the turtle cross the road?

A. To get to the Shell Station.

Q: What do little monkeys have with their milk?

A: Chocolate chimp cookies.

Q: What do frogs eat with their hamburgers?

A: French flies.

Q. What time is it when you go to the dentist?

A. Tooth-hurty.

Q: What is a little dog's favorite drink?

A: Pup-si Cola.

Q: Did you hear about the man who lost his entire left side?

A: He's all-right now.

Q: What do you call the ghost who haunts a TV talk show?

A: Phantom of the Oprah.

Q. What did the daddy buffalo say to his boy as youngster left for school?

A. "Bye, son."

Q: What kind of illness does Jackie Chan have?

A: Kung Flu.

Q: What kind of bread spread do cars make?

A: Traffic jam.

Q. Why didn't the oyster give up her pearl?

A. She was shellfish.

Q: What do you call the elephant witch doctor?

A: Mumbo Jumbo.

KNOCK KNOCK JOKES

Knock, knock.

Who's there?

Hatch.

Hatch who?

Are you catching a cold?

Knock, knock.

Who's there?

Alex.

Alex who?

Alex the questions around here!

Knock, knock.

Who's there?

Thistle.

Thistle who?

Thistle have to hold you until dinner's ready.

Knock, knock.

Who's there?

Duane.

Duane who?

Duane the bathtub—I'm dwowning!

Knock, knock.

Who's there?

Little old lady.

Little old lady who?

Wow! I didn't know you could yodel.

Knock, knock.

Who's there?

Pecan.

Pecan who?

Pecan someone your own size!

Knock, knock.

Who's there?

Lena.

Lena who?

Lena little closer, I want to tell you a secret.

Knock, knock.

Who's there?

Fish.

Fish who?

Fish you a Merry Christmas, we fish you a Merry Christmas.

Knock, knock.

Who's there?

Police.

Police who?

Police stop telling these awful knock-knock jokes!

<hr />

and for the adults among us . . .

Knock, knock.

Who's there?

Catgut.

Catgut who?

Catgut your tongue?

Knock, knock.

Who's there?

Wendy.

Wendy who?

Wendy Red Red Robin Comes Bob Bob Bobbin' Along . . .

Knock, knock.

Who's there?

Aaron.

Aaron who?

Always Aaron the side of caution!

Knock, knock.

Who's there?

Franz.

Franz who?

Franz, Romans, Countrymen . . . !

YO' MAMA JOKES

Yo' mama is so fat . . .

She was baptized at Sea World.

When she gets on a scale, it says, "To be continued . . ."

Her belt size is "Equator."

She uses a boomerang to put on a belt.

When she wears a yellow raincoat, people yell, "Taxi!"

She's once, twice, three times a lady.

Her blood type is Ragu.

I had to take a train and two buses just to get on her good side.

She eats "Wheat Thicks."

The bathroom scale reads, "One at a time, please."

When she sits around the house, she sits *around* the house.

Yo' mama is so ugly . . .

She trick or treats on the phone.

Your father takes her to work with him so that he doesn't have to kiss her goodbye.

She turned Medusa to stone.

She tried to enter an ugly contest, but was told it wasn't open to professionals.

They filmed *Gorillas in the Mist* in her shower.

Her mama had to tie a steak around her neck to get the dog to play with her.

When she was born, the doctor slapped her face.

When she was born, the doctor slapped her mother's face.

Yo' Mama is so dumb . . .

She took the Pepsi Challenge and chose Coca-Cola.

She saw a sign that said "Wet Floor," so she did.

When asked on an application, "Sex?" she marked, "M, F and sometimes Wednesdays."

She cooks Indian curry with Old Spice.

She thought that TuPac Shakur was a Jewish holiday.

When she went to the movies, and saw a sign that said "under 17 not admitted," she went home and got 16 friends.

When she heard that 90% of all crimes occur in the home, she moved.

She thinks Cheerios are doughnut seeds.

When you were born, she looked at your umbilical cord and said, "Wow, it comes with cable!"

INDEX